I CAN DRAW
CARTOONS

A step-by-step introduction to drawing fantastic cartoons

Paul B. Davies • Kevin Faerber
Terry Longhurst • David Pattison

Text by Amanda O'Neill

p

This is a Parragon Publishing Book
This edition published in 2004

Parragon Publishing
Queen Street House
4 Queen Street
Bath BA1 1HE, UK

Copyright © Parragon 2001

Designed, produced and packaged by
Stonecastle Graphics Limited
Cover design by Seagull

Designed by Paul Turner and Sue Pressley
Edited by Philip de Ste. Croix

ISBN 1-40540-542-2

Printed in China

About This Book

CARTOONS are drawings which take a humorous look at the world. They are fun to look at, and they are fun to draw. This book shows you how to create a host of entertaining characters, building up your drawings in easy stages.

The tools you need are simple – paper, a selection of pencils, and an eraser. Fairly thick paper is best to work with (very thin paper wears through if you have to rub out a line).

To color in your drawings, you can use paints, crayons, colored inks, or felt-tip pens. Fine felt-tips are useful for drawing outlines, while thick ones are better for coloring in.

Remember that cartoons aren't meant to be realistic. They are imaginative and exaggerated. You can draw monsters or fairies, create cute animals or fearsome dinosaurs, or even give a cartoon character a nose that is bigger than his feet. Anything is possible in cartoon-land.

But they are meant to be recognizable. You need to get inside your subject just as much as if you were making an accurate portrait. Most cartoons take some feature of the subject and exaggerate it to comic effect. So you need to decide which feature you want to emphasize. It may be the way your subject stands, or moves. It may be big feet or a funny expression.

The step-by-step drawings in this book will give you plenty of ideas to get you started. After that, there's a whole world out there to draw!

Big-Ears the Elephant

From Babar to Dumbo, not forgetting Hathi in *The Jungle Book*, cartoonists have loved elephants. You may also be inspired by early Western pictures of elephants by artists who had never seen one, but only heard descriptions.

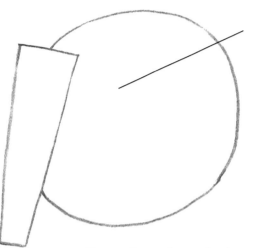

Start with these two shapes — a rough circle for the huge body, and a long, four-sided shape for the head and trunk.

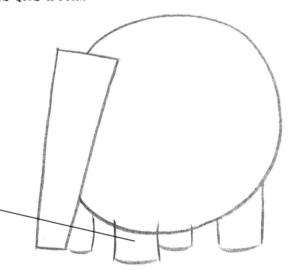

Draw four short, thick legs. By making them much shorter than in real life, you make the body look even bigger.

Draw two large arch-shaped ears, reaching from the top of the head to halfway down.

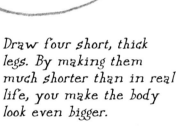

Add round eyes, about a third of the way down the head, and a simple tusk just below the ear.

A couple of raised eyebrows create a surprised expression. Don't forget to add a tail at the other end.

What is green and has a trunk?

An elephant that's been picked too soon.

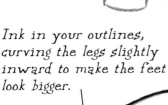

Ink in your outlines, curving the legs slightly inward to make the feet look bigger.

Now you can shape the head, rounding the forehead and making the trunk bulge, then taper. Make the lower edges of the ears rough and floppy.

Use light and dark shading to make your elephant look really solid. The dark shadow on the ground gives a great impression of size and weight

What do you get if you cross an elephant with peanut butter?

A spread that never forgets!

Lofty the Giraffe

The giraffe is a walking watchtower! His great height helps him see for miles across the savannah, so no enemy can sneak up on him.

Draw a long, flattened oval for the head.

Now draw a big blobby nose on top of the head, at the end.

This long spike forms the neck. Extend it across the head and just beyond. The point at the top will show you where to put the eyes!

These two little circles will form the knobs on the end of the horns. Start a little way inward from the back of the head.

Using the point of the neck 'spike' as a guide, draw two eyes perched on top of the head. Behind them, draw the horns.

Now add two long ears, shaped like leaves and laid flat on either side of the eyes.

Shape the neck where it joins the head, and hollow out the underside of the jaw. A tufty fringe round the eyes gives character to the head.

Draw in the bristly mane, and spots, and give your giraffe a leaf to munch.

That long neck makes a great periscope — but imagine being a giraffe with a sore throat!

Honey Bear

Bears love honey. In the wild, they have to rob bees' nests to get it, and usually get well stung in the process. For cartoon bears, life is easier because honey comes in jars. All this bear has to worry about is finding a comfortable place to enjoy his feast!

Start with a big egg shape for the body, and add a rounded nose near the top.

Add a couple of round ears at the top, and — most important! — this shape for the honey jar.

Now add two big feet, on short legs.

Draw in the curved arm, and the edge of a paw clutching the honey jar.

Two small round eyes go just at the top of the head.

Now you can put in the facial features. The little tongue peeps out of the mouth in anticipation.

Finish your outline, and label the honey jar with a picture of a bee. Add a shiny highlight to the big, black nose.

What do Baloo the Bear and Winnie the Pooh have in common?

Their middle names!

Porky Pig

Our view of pigs is strange. We are often rather rude about them — 'dirty pigs' and 'greedy swine.' Yet, at the same time, we find their comfortable round shape rather appealing, so we enjoy toy pigs, cartoon pigs — and, of course, piggy banks.

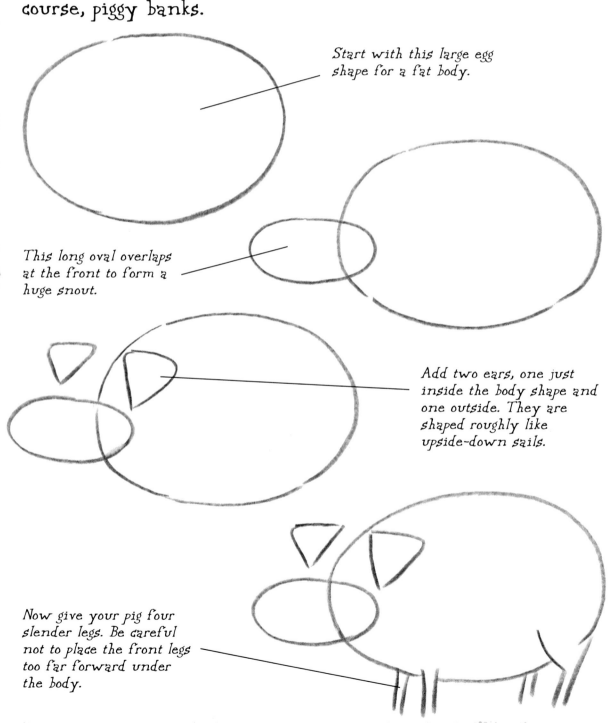

Start with this large egg shape for a fat body.

This long oval overlaps at the front to form a huge snout.

Add two ears, one just inside the body shape and one outside. They are shaped roughly like upside-down sails.

Now give your pig four slender legs. Be careful not to place the front legs too far forward under the body.

Fill in the face around the snout and ears. Add a gentle curve stretching from in front of the forelegs to beneath the snout, to form the chest and neck.

Finish the head with two little piggy eyes and a couple of wide-spaced nostrils. They make Porky look vaguely surprised

Pigs like their comfort, so draw in a shelter.

Why don't piglets ever listen to their father?

Because they find him such a boar!

You can color your pig pink, or banded, or spotted, depending on your taste. A dappling of spots helps to make him look more solidly rounded.

Cool Camel

The 'ship of the desert' is famous for two things. One is its 'backpack,' the hump in which it keeps emergency supplies for desert life. The other is its sneer. Few people can sneer half as well as a camel — our mouths aren't made for it.

Start with these two simple shapes (head and hump), taking care to space them the right distance apart.

Two curving lines linking your first two shapes form a thick, strong neck and chest.

Add on legs and hindquarters. Now you can see that the big egg shape forms a round tummy as well as the hump.

Finish off the legs with big, sandshoe feet, and add a cheerful little tail.

Top off the head with eyes, a rounded forehead, and an ear. Sketch in knobbly knees.

Grown the hump with a jagged-edged topping to represent shaggy hair.

Ink in the outlines, bringing out the curves a little more. Add a sticking plaster to our poor, tired old friend.

A little pyramid in the background will help to make your camel feel at home.

Mole in a Hole

Living underground, the mole doesn't need good eyesight: he is nearly blind. What he does need is good digging tools, so he has huge hands which he uses like spades. He is drawn here peeping out of his molehill — he wouldn't be happy away from it.

Start with these two shapes — the molehill, and a 'shark's fin' shape for the mole's head.

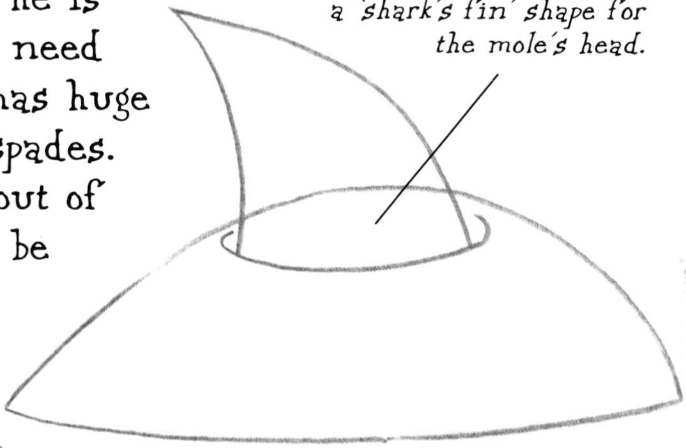

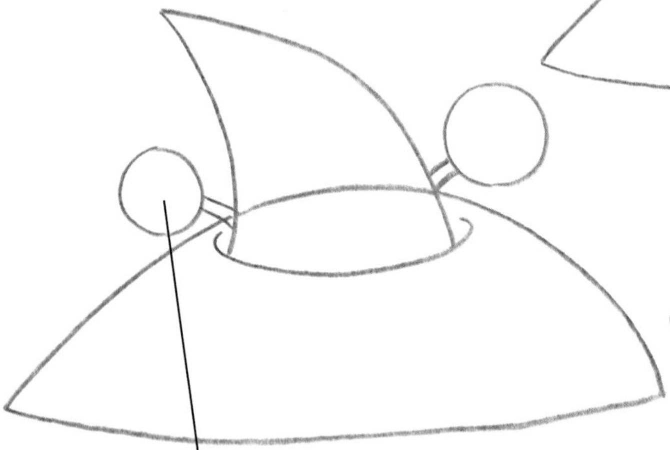

Four small circles form nose, eyes, and an ear.

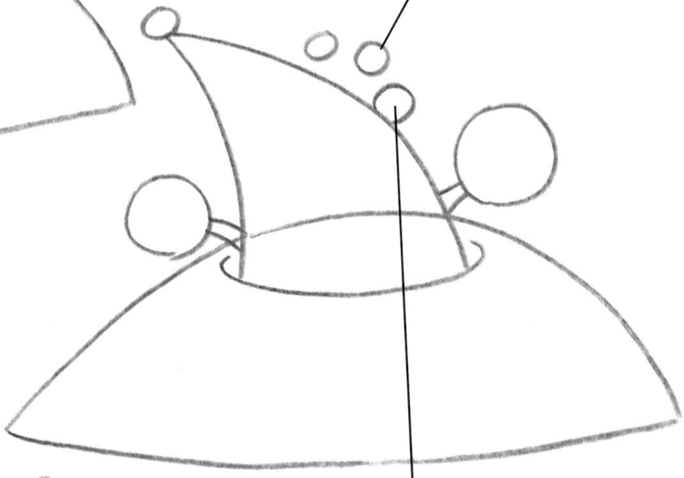

Add two thin little arms, ending in big circles as guidelines for the mole's large hands.

Take care with the spacing of these circles.

The hands become bigger when you add fat, sausage-like fingers and thumbs. Join the two eye circles, and add a curved arm to make them into eyeglasses sitting just above the face.

Give your mole a small, smiley mouth — about halfway down the 'shark's fin' shape.

Start inking in your outlines. Add a few whiskers around the nose. Use a bold curving line to mark out the lighter-colored chest fur — the mole's 'velvet waistcoat.'

Finish off your drawing by turning the mound into a real molehill, with lumps and bumps and rough edges. A few tiny clods of earth flying from the mole's outstretched hands show that work is in progress!

Moles seem to delight in throwing up their hills in the middle of the smoothest lawns, or the most carefully tended flower beds. You may like to draw some collapsing flowers round the mound.

Mrs Kangaroo

Kangaroos, of course, are famous for having invented the pocket and turned it into a portable nursery. Mind you, it's tough on a kangaroo mother. As she says, 'I hate it when it's raining and the kids have to play inside!'

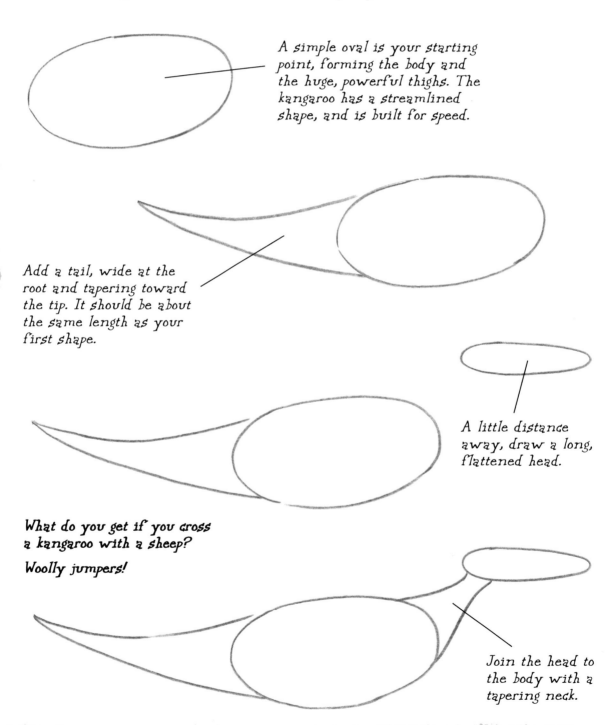

A simple oval is your starting point, forming the body and the huge, powerful thighs. The kangaroo has a streamlined shape, and is built for speed.

Add a tail, wide at the root and tapering toward the tip. It should be about the same length as your first shape.

A little distance away, draw a long, flattened head.

What do you get if you cross a kangaroo with a sheep?

Woolly jumpers!

Join the head to the body with a tapering neck.

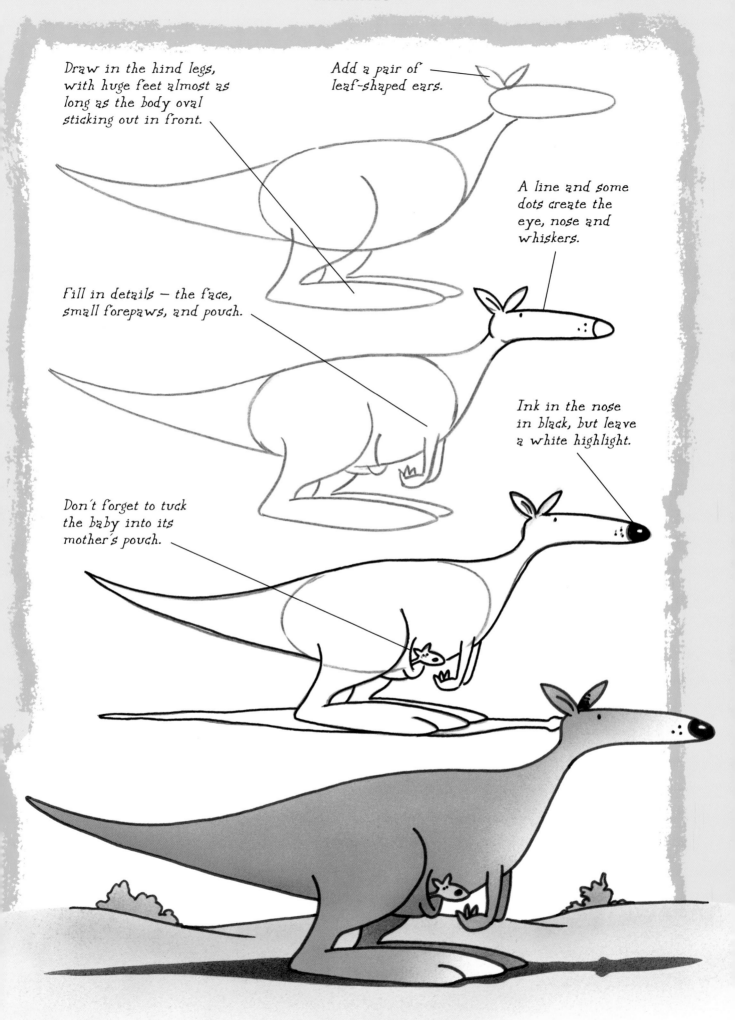

Draw in the hind legs, with huge feet almost as long as the body oval sticking out in front.

Add a pair of leaf-shaped ears.

A line and some dots create the eye, nose and whiskers.

Fill in details — the face, small forepaws, and pouch.

Ink in the nose in black, but leave a white highlight.

Don't forget to tuck the baby into its mother's pouch.

Pretty Polly!

Parrots are noted for their beautiful colors and their ability to talk. Just as striking is the parrot's beak, which serves as a multi-purpose tool-kit — nutcracker, pliers, grappling hook, etc. Its size and shape make this beak a cartoonist's dream.

Two simple shapes start you off — a circle topped by a 'dunce cap.'

Add a big curved shape for the beak, and two small circles for the feet.

Now add the wing, shaped like a long leaf and roughly twice the length of the circle.

The tail is nearly as long as the wing, and grows wider toward the end.

Give your parrot a perch to sit on, and add a large eye and a crest on top of the head.

Shape the head, curving the neck and forming a sharp, hook-shaped beak.

Fill in details — feathers, toes, etc. — and don't forget the food bowl.

You can have fun with the colors. There are more than 300 varieties of parrots, so that should give you plenty to choose from!

What does a mathematician call a dead parrot?

A polygon!

Hockey Player

Movements are exaggerated in the cartoon world. So an awkward lunge at the ball in real life becomes very awkward indeed when we draw it. Making the hockey player squat and chunky, rather than fit and lean, emphasizes the comic effect.

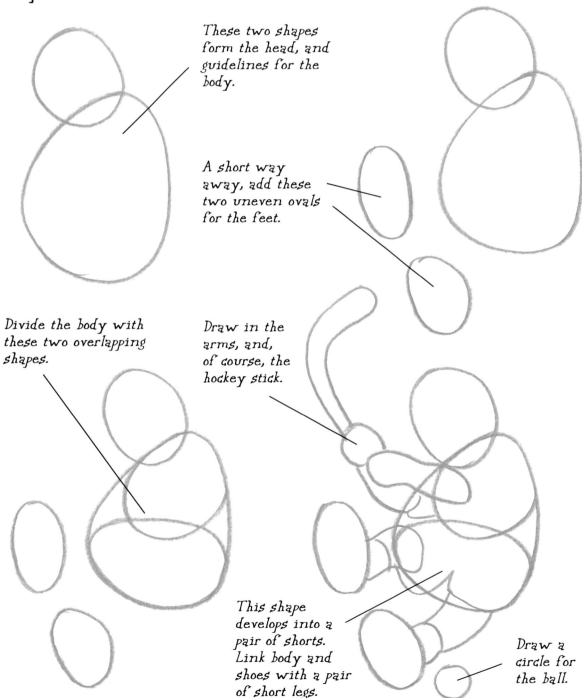

These two shapes form the head, and guidelines for the body.

A short way away, add these two uneven ovals for the feet.

Divide the body with these two overlapping shapes.

Draw in the arms, and, of course, the hockey stick.

This shape develops into a pair of shorts. Link body and shoes with a pair of short legs.

Draw a circle for the ball.

Draw in hair and face. A lopsided mouth gives a look of intense concentration.

Start to ink in your outlines.

Shirt and shorts are made up of a series of simple curves.

The hands are simplified — cartoon characters often have only three fingers like this.

Little bows on the clumpy shoes add a comic touch.

Ice Skater

Drawing someone who is ill-suited to their chosen sport, like a small, weedy weightlifter, is another way of making a comic picture. Here we have a skater with all the grace of a hippopotamus!

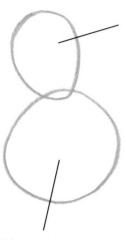

Start with an egg shape for the head.

This circle forms the chubby body.

Position this large oval overlapping the body circle just below the center. Believe it or not, this is nearly all the guideline you need for the legs!

Position the feet. One just overlaps the lower shape, and the other is its own length below it.

When you draw in hair, plump arms, and huge, wobbly legs, the whole figure starts to appear.

Draw the face, leaving plenty of room for a nice set of double chins.

The arms are raised in what would be a graceful arch if they were more shapely.

Draw the skirt hem as a wavy line that spreads out beyond her fat thighs.

Make the skates big and rather shapeless — not for dainty little feet!

Add a few broken rings to show the skate marks — and let's hope she isn't skating on thin ice!

Where does a mouse go to skate?

The mice rink!

Soccer Player

We call it soccer or football — but one of its high points might well be called headball! Action pictures are always fun to draw. Here we have a soccer star caught at the moment when he leaps into the air to head the ball.

Start with these two egg shapes, for the head and chest. Don't forget to leave a space between them for a neck.

This shape, rather like the cap of a toadstool, is placed off-center at the base of the chest, and will form the tops of the legs.

Add a circle for the ball, just above the player's head.

This arm stretches out. For the other arm, only the hand and wrist extend beyond your oval shape.

Three more shapes complete the outline of the bent legs. Only one foot is visible at this angle.

Because his head is tipped back toward the ball, set the features high on the face, with the smiling mouth roughly at the center.

An extra curve makes his football shirt swing loosely out from his body, increasing the impression of movement.

Some symmetrical lines make up the sections of the football.

Football boots don't need a lot of definition. Just add a simple pattern and laces — and the essential studs.

Choose the shirt color of your favorite team, or make up one of your own.

What did the fairy godfather promise?

'Yes, Cinderella, you shall go to the football!'

Diver

Water gives us a lot of images in everyday speech. We say that people 'dive into' things when they are keen, or 'dip a toe in the water' when they are slow and cautious. Faced with real water, this diver is managing to do both!

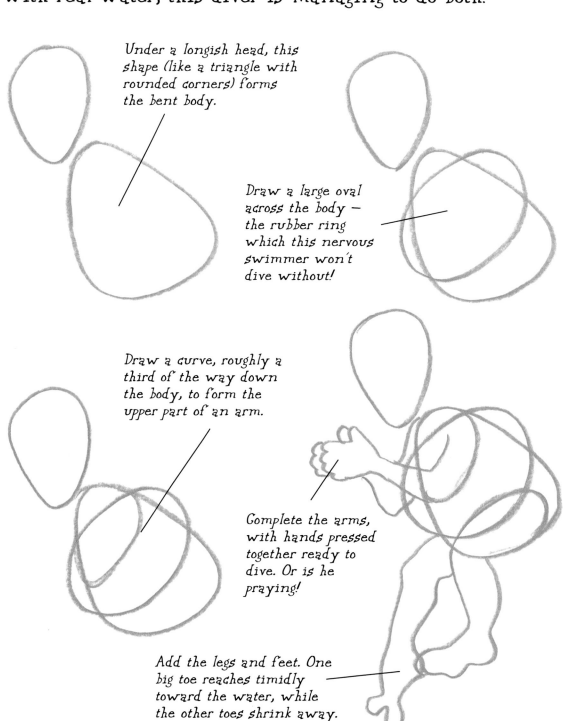

Under a longish head, this shape (like a triangle with rounded corners) forms the bent body.

Draw a large oval across the body — the rubber ring which this nervous swimmer won't dive without!

Draw a curve, roughly a third of the way down the body, to form the upper part of an arm.

Complete the arms, with hands pressed together ready to dive. Or is he praying!

Add the legs and feet. One big toe reaches timidly toward the water, while the other toes shrink away.

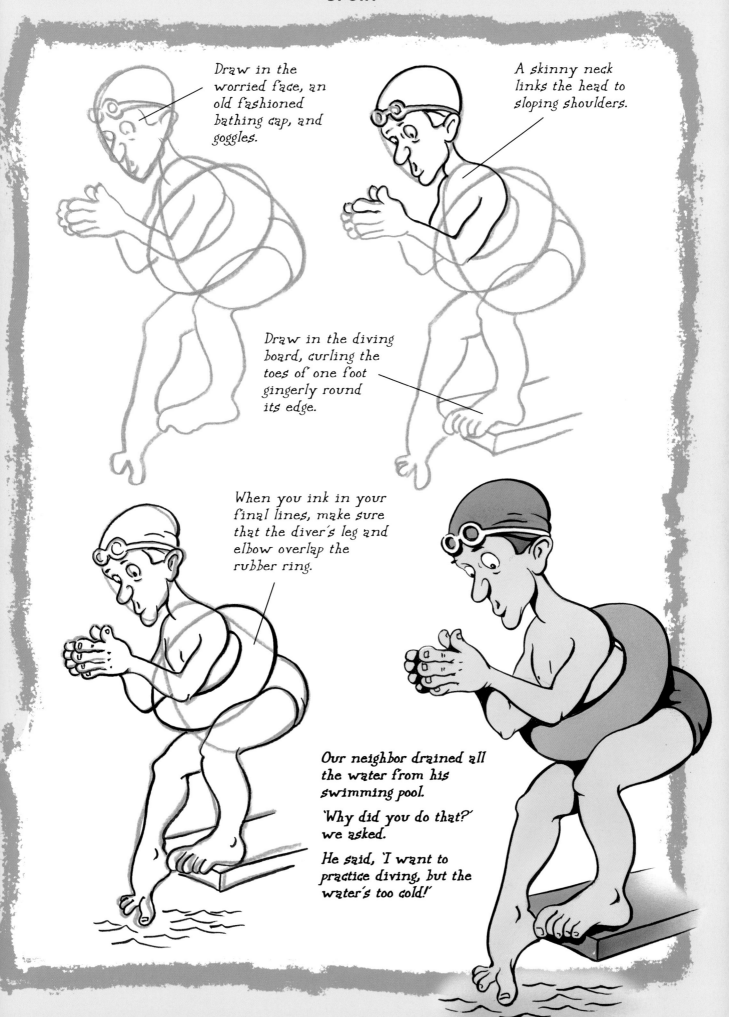

Draw in the worried face, an old fashioned bathing cap, and goggles.

A skinny neck links the head to sloping shoulders.

Draw in the diving board, curling the toes of one foot gingerly round its edge.

When you ink in your final lines, make sure that the diver's leg and elbow overlap the rubber ring.

Our neighbor drained all the water from his swimming pool.

'Why did you do that?' we asked.

He said, 'I want to practice diving, but the water's too cold!'

Weightlifter

Weightlifting is an increasingly popular form of exercise today. Not all weightlifters are muscle-bound hunks who strain at huge weights. Here we have one who is really enjoying herself — watch out, Wondergirl!

Start with the head and body, slightly overlapping one another.

Leave a space between the body and the arms, where you can draw in sleeves later.

Draw the thighs as two longish ovals at the base of the figure.

Draw this weight round, and the one at the other end oval.

Shape the upper body, curving it inward to a trim waist.

Wiggly lines for the legs prepare the way for folds in the tracksuit botoms.

Use jagged lines to form a mane of shaggy hair behind a sweatband.

Add creases to the sleeves and waist of the T-shirt.

The curved bar of the weights is reflected in the curve of the weightlifter's thighs. This creates a balance between the top and bottom of the drawing.

Curve the arms slightly at the elbows. The big smile tells it all!

Skier

When things go wrong on the sports field, the cartoonist leaps in with glee. But someone having a good time enjoying their favorite sport can also make a great cartoon. All you have to do is exaggerate a little!

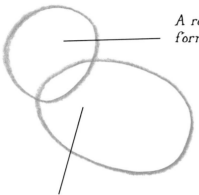

A rough circle forms the head.

Extend this shape (shoulder and arm) down almost to the lower edge of the body.

Overlapping the edge of the head, the body leans at an angle to crouch over the skis.

Add a raised arm. Draw a large shape for the hand, because of the thick gloves.

One ski stick waves joyfully in the air, while the other is tucked under the other arm.

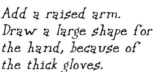

These two shapes for the thighs slant slightly upward toward the back of the body.

The large feet extend beyond each knee, and are set into bindings on narrow skis.

Draw the face, with a wide happy grin. In real life, the shades would cover his eyes — but we want to be able to see his gleeful expression.

Curved creases in his ski pants suggest the shape of the legs beneath. Add some more creases in his jacket as well.

Curly hair is easy to draw, with lots of small bubbly curves.

Skiing is easy. You can learn how to do it in just a few sittings!

Basketball Player

All sorts of things can go wrong on the basketball court. Here, the idea is to get the ball in the basket. However, it seems this player has got it all wrong. Either that, or he must be a bit of a basket case!

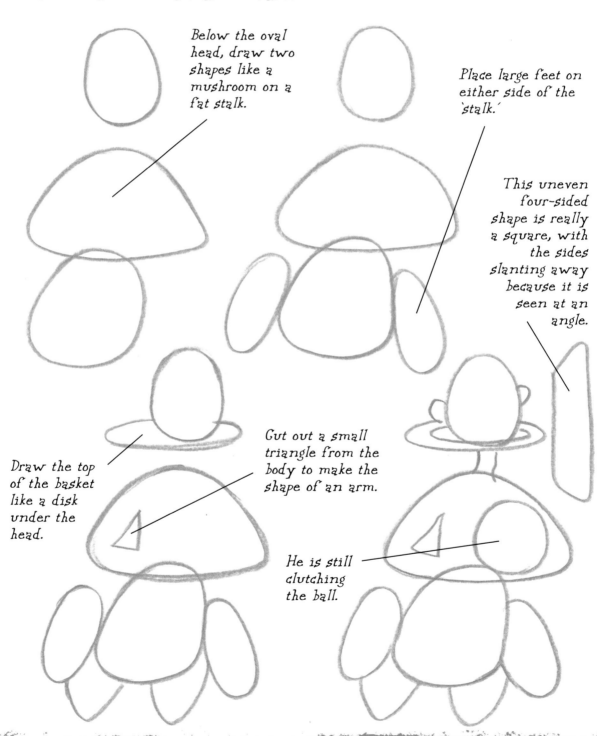

Below the oval head, draw two shapes like a mushroom on a fat stalk.

Place large feet on either side of the 'stalk.'

This uneven four-sided shape is really a square, with the sides slanting away because it is seen at an angle.

Draw the top of the basket like a disk under the head.

Cut out a small triangle from the body to make the shape of an arm.

He is still clutching the ball.

Draw in his face. The wide eyes and down-turned mouth say 'Whoa!'

The net of the basket bulges outward round its unlikely catch.

Sketch in the pattern of his sneakers.

A short stem attaches the basket to the backboard on the wall.

Large hands clutch the ball in an embarrassed grip.

His legs are tucked up in a great leap. Try a slam dunk next time!

Golfer

Golf takes a lot of concentration. Watch a golfer studying his ball, choosing his line, and finally making a swing, and you will find many opportunities for cartoons. The amount of effort going into this shot is staggering, in all senses!

Start with this snowman shape, tipping the head to one side.

Two ovals create the legs. Slant them at slightly different angles.

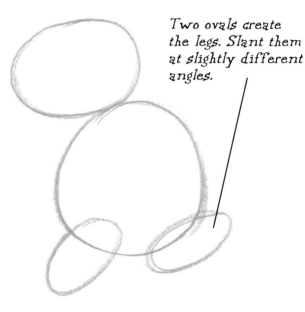

A curve between head and body begins to form a raised arm.

The power of his swing takes his golf club right behind his head.

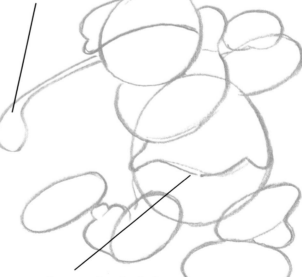

Complete this leg with a rounded blob for the shin, and a raised foot above it.

A wavy line a third of the way up his body marks the bottom of his waistcoat.

Draw in his face. Three short curving lines form one eye screwed shut in concentration, while the other eye is wide and round.

His fingers are curled tightly round the handle of the golf club.

The loose trousers fall into curves and folds before tucking into the socks. The ankles are comically thin above large golf shoes.

When the doctor told my father to go out and play thirty-six holes a day, I don't think he understood.

Pop went out and bought a harmonica!

Cupid

The Roman god of love, Cupid, is a mischievous child. He shoots his golden arrows at people to make them fall in love, often choosing the most unlikely couples, just for fun. Today we still use images of Cupid on Valentine's cards.

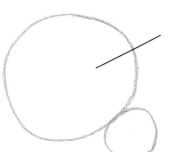

Start with a large circle for the head, and a smaller one which will make the front part of the body.

Position these two small circles, for the hands, carefully, the left one a little lower than the right.

Add another circle, slightly overlapping the first body section and just a little smaller.

Two small ovals, overlapping the second body section, make Cupid's thighs. Little arms link the hands to the body, and two more small circles, low on the face, form chubby cheeks.

Cupid's natural habitat is in the heavens, so add a couple of clouds.

Draw in the face, placing the nose between the round cheeks and eyes just above them. Add a pair of small wings, complete the legs, and don't forget Cupid's bow.

Start filling in details: Cupid's curly hair, his hands, and wing feathers running in two rows.

Finish drawing the face, giving Cupid an expression of cheeky mischief.

Draw the arrow just leaving the bow. Cupid's left hand has only just fired it, so indicate the hand's movement with a couple of little curved 'spin marks' in front of it.

Use curved 'spin marks' again to indicate movement, this time of Cupid's wings.

The two cheek circles form guidelines for the placement and spacing of his other features.

Cupid's head is drawn much bigger than his body. Sometimes he is drawn without any body at all — just a head, wings and, of course, hands to hold his golden bow.

Supergirl

Many fantasy figures, like dragons and fairies, date back for centuries. But fantasy isn't stuck in the past. Comic-strip heroes and heroines with super-powers are part of a thriving modern fantasy tradition.

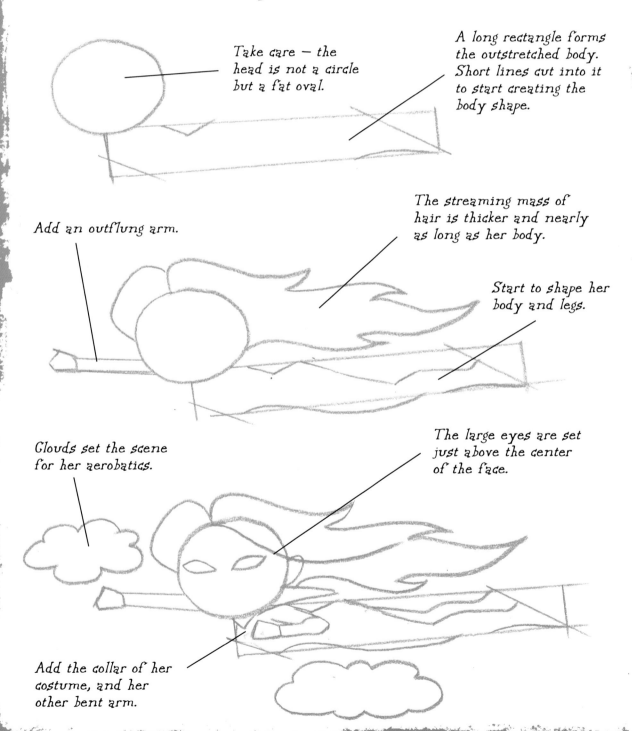

Take care — the head is not a circle but a fat oval.

A long rectangle forms the outstretched body. Short lines cut into it to start creating the body shape.

Add an outflung arm.

The streaming mass of hair is thicker and nearly as long as her body.

Start to shape her body and legs.

Clouds set the scene for her aerobatics.

The large eyes are set just above the center of the face.

Add the collar of her costume, and her other bent arm.

Finish drawing the face. Large features occupy almost all the space.

Complete the feet with a cool pair of boots.

Dimples at the corners of the mouth create a more natural smile than curving the lips.

Her costume is easily sketched in with a few curved lines.

The hands are drawn as closed fists punching through the air.

A few short 'speed lines' behind the figure increase the impression of movement.

Supergirl to the rescue!

Tree Goblin

An old rhyme tells us that 'Fairy folks are in old oaks,' and who knows what lives hidden among the trees? This goblin is small enough to wear an acorn cup as a hat, so he would be very hard to spot in his leafy home.

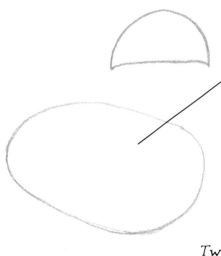

Start with a small half-circle for the acorn-cup hat and, below, a big blobby oval for the goblin's body.

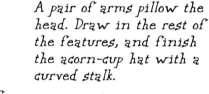

Curved lines will make the shape of the face.

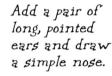

Two small, rough circles mark out the positions of his feet.

Above each foot circle, add a slanting shape for the big toe.

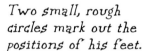

Add a pair of long, pointed ears and draw a simple nose.

A pair of arms pillow the head. Draw in the rest of the features, and finish the acorn-cup hat with a curved stalk.

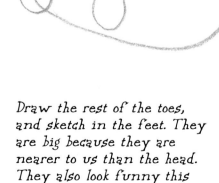

Draw the rest of the toes, and sketch in the feet. They are big because they are nearer to us than the head. They also look funny this way!

Fill in the body shape with pointed leaves.

Use simple curved lines for closed eyes. A blissful smile takes up nearly the full width of the face.

Sketch in the lines of branches around the goblin, arranging them so that they form a comfortable nest for him.

A leafy blanket covers the goblin from chin to ankles. Add scratchy lines across the branches of his nest to give the effect of rough bark.

Why didn't the goblin wake up for dinner?

The cook didn't use elf-raising flour!

(Mind you, gobblin' your dinner is bad for your elf!)

Mermaid

Tales of mermaids — half fish, half woman — have been told since ancient times. They are always beautiful, with flowing hair and sweet voices. This is odd, since scientists say the legend was probably inspired by the manatee, or sea cow, a rather unlovely beast!

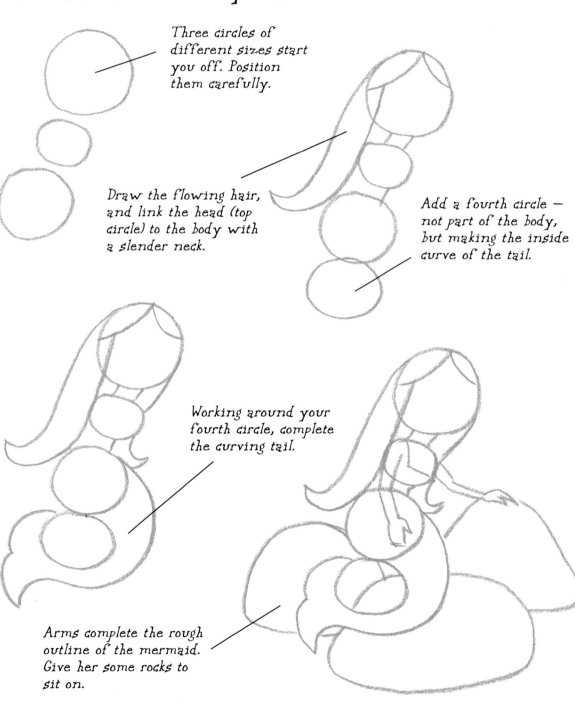

Three circles of different sizes start you off. Position them carefully.

Draw the flowing hair, and link the head (top circle) to the body with a slender neck.

Add a fourth circle — not part of the body, but making the inside curve of the tail.

Working around your fourth circle, complete the curving tail.

Arms complete the rough outline of the mermaid. Give her some rocks to sit on.

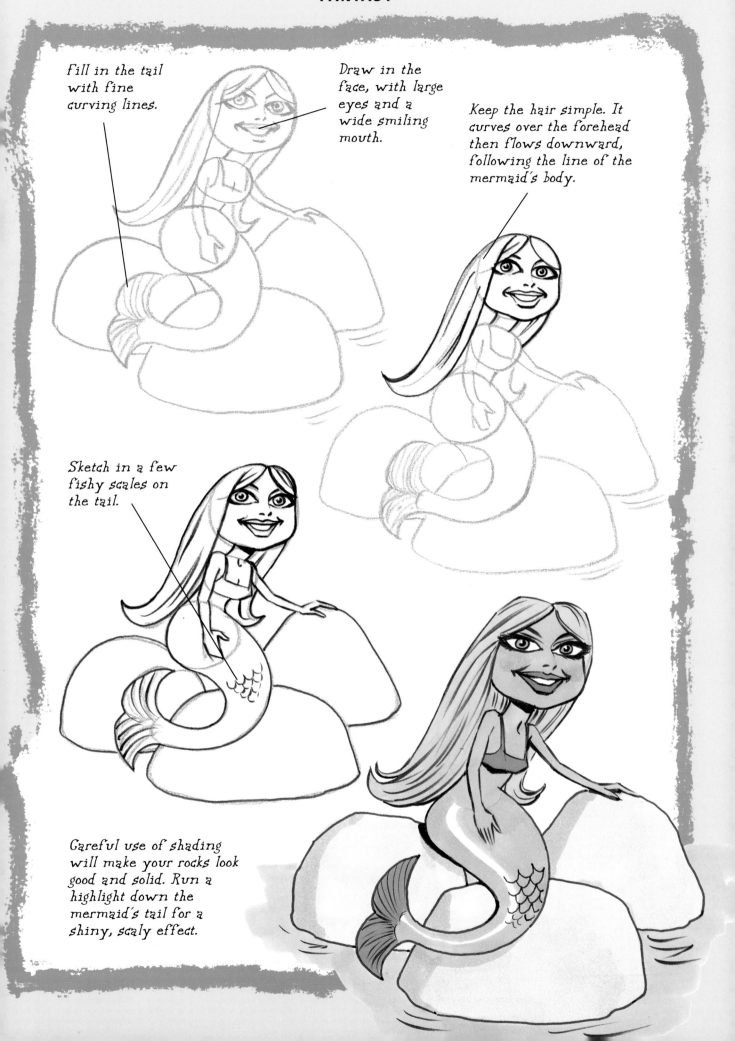

Fill in the tail with fine curving lines.

Draw in the face, with large eyes and a wide smiling mouth.

Keep the hair simple. It curves over the forehead then flows downward, following the line of the mermaid's body.

Sketch in a few fishy scales on the tail.

Careful use of shading will make your rocks look good and solid. Run a highlight down the mermaid's tail for a shiny, scaly effect.

Leprechaun

The Leprechaun — a merry little fellow dressed in green — is the fairy shoemaker of Ireland. If you can catch him, you can demand his secret hoard of gold as the price of his freedom — but he will nearly always manage to escape without paying up.

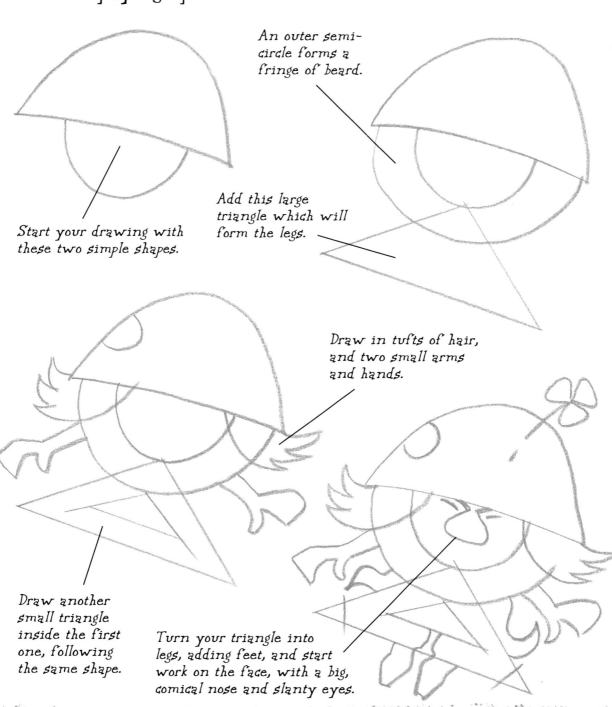

An outer semi-circle forms a fringe of beard.

Start your drawing with these two simple shapes.

Add this large triangle which will form the legs.

Draw in tufts of hair, and two small arms and hands.

Draw another small triangle inside the first one, following the same shape.

Turn your triangle into legs, adding feet, and start work on the face, with a big, comical nose and slanty eyes.

Take a 'bite' out of the hat.

Finish the face with a big, buck-toothed grin, taking the smile lines up to the sides of the nose.

A true Irishman, the Leprechaun has tucked a leaf of Ireland's national plant, the shamrock, into his hat.

Sketch in trousers, creased behind the knee, stockings, and a pair of smart buckled shoes, fit for a champion shoemaker.

Make the hair and beard look suitably 'wild and woolly.'

Notice that you didn't need to draw the Leprechaun's body, only his legs. Hidden by his beard, it is suggested by his flying coat-tails.

Centaur

Centaurs — half man and half horse — belong to ancient legend. They are often said to be great hunters, skilled with bow and arrow. This is why the star sign Sagittarius, 'the Archer,' is usually shown in pictures as a centaur.

These two shapes form the human half of the centaur — head and chest.

The horse's body is formed by a shape similar to the head, but lying on its side.

Divide the face with lines, to help you place the features. Add a mane of hair.

The guidelines give you the positions of eyes, nose, and mouth, as well as mustache and eyebrows.

Draw the centaur's bow.

Add a flowing tail.

Small circles will help you to draw the legs.

A quiver of arrows hangs behind his back, the strap running across his chest.

Thick, boldly curved eyebrows and a full beard give his face a fierce expression.

Marking the joints with circles helps you to shape the legs and hoofs.

Tidy up your outlines as you ink them in.

Have a go at drawing other mythical mixtures — like the griffin, half eagle, half lion!

Magic Carpet

Tales of flying carpets come from the East, where beautiful carpets are woven. This might be a rather drafty form of transport, probably best in hot, dry climates. In rainy weather most of us would prefer an airplane!

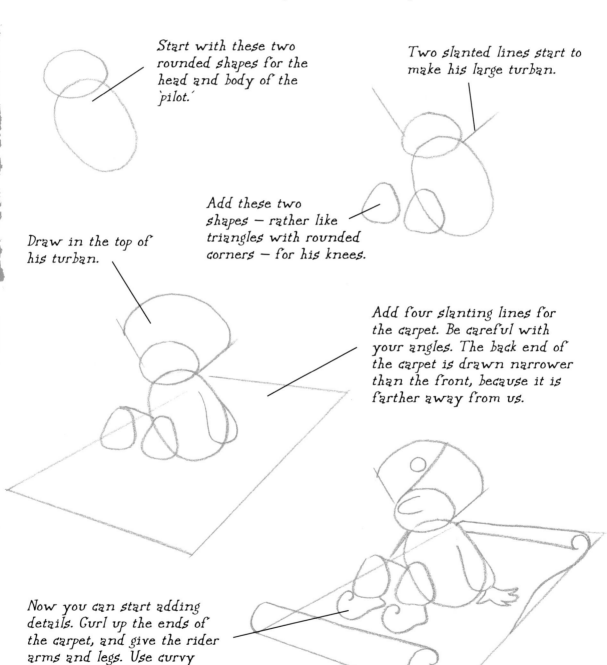

Start with these two rounded shapes for the head and body of the 'pilot.'

Two slanted lines start to make his large turban.

Add these two shapes — rather like triangles with rounded corners — for his knees.

Draw in the top of his turban.

Add four slanting lines for the carpet. Be careful with your angles. The back end of the carpet is drawn narrower than the front, because it is farther away from us.

Now you can start adding details. Curl up the ends of the carpet, and give the rider arms and legs. Use curvy lines for his feet, which wear slippers with long, curling toes.

Fill in the face. Round staring eyes make the carpet's rider look just a little bit worried, despite his smile. It's a long way down!

Finish drawing his head, adding a little fringe of beard. A large and splendid ornament fastens his turban.

The turban looks better with a few folds in the cloth, shown by little curving lines.

Clouds help to set the scene up in the sky.

Unlike real life, cartoon people always wear clothes that show exactly who they are. Cooks wear chefs' hats, burglars wear striped jerseys — and flying carpet riders wear full Eastern costume.

Vampire

Horror-story vampires are scary creatures with creepy clothes. Real-life vampires are just bats. They have nothing in common except drinking blood. Our cartoon vampire combines the two: his cloak suggests a bat's wings and tail.

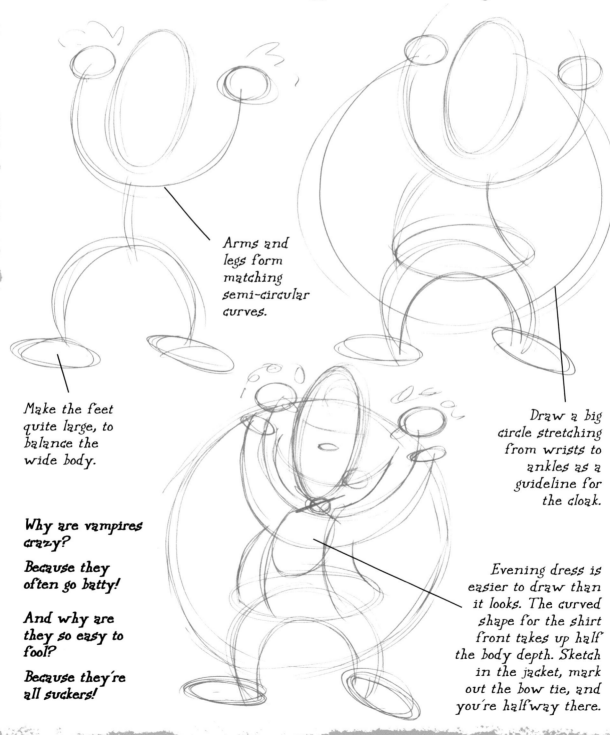

Arms and legs form matching semi-circular curves.

Make the feet quite large, to balance the wide body.

Draw a big circle stretching from wrists to ankles as a guideline for the cloak.

Why are vampires crazy?

Because they often go batty!

And why are they so easy to fool?

Because they're all suckers!

Evening dress is easier to draw than it looks. The curved shape for the shirt front takes up half the body depth. Sketch in the jacket, mark out the bow tie, and you're halfway there.

Draw in the face, filling the lower half with an evil smile. The ear is very low-set for comic effect.

A single eyebrow is the popular style among creatures of the night like vampires and werewolves.

Draw the spread fingers all round the hand for a claw-like effect.

No vampire is complete without his fangs. Very tasty.

What does a polite vampire say after he's bitten you?

'Fangs a lot!'

Werewolf

Werewolves in old stories are scary, because they change shape so convincingly. Anyone might be a werewolf in human form! Modern versions often forget to lose the hair and teeth when they become human — the cartoon kind more than most!

Plan where the eyes will be.

Start with an egg for the head, and add on these curves and ovals for the body and legs.

Even a hand can be built up with added ovals, which will form clutching fingers and thumb.

Curved lines form a skinny arm.

These oval shapes will give you the rough outline of your werewolf's shaggy mane.

I used to be a werewolf, but I'm all right nooooooow!

Start building up the face, feature by feature. Sketch small circles under the eyes to help build up the muzzle beyond the human shape.

Use eye shape to express the mood of your character. These round eyes create a comic look, where long narrow eyes would look more sinister.

A few short lines sketch in hair on the arms.

What big teeth you have, Grandmother! Remember to draw longer canine teeth at the corners of the mouth.

Head hair stretches down the back in a shaggy mane.

Tip fingers and thumbs with claws.

The contrast between the monstrous front part of the beast and the weedy little legs adds to the humor of the drawing.

Fluff

Have you ever wondered about those bits of fluff under the bed? Supposing they were alive, what would they look like? Here's one idea. Fluff is only small, but are you sure you want him lurking under your bed? Perhaps it's time to clean!

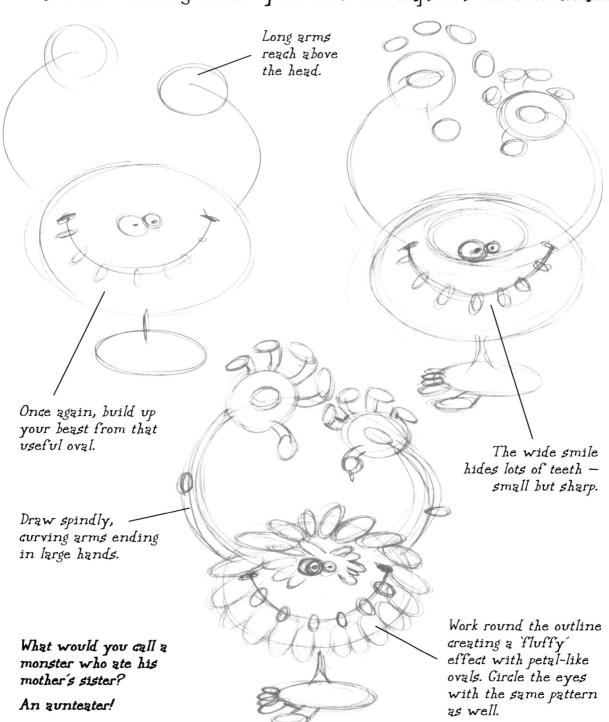

Long arms reach above the head.

Once again, build up your beast from that useful oval.

Draw spindly, curving arms ending in large hands.

The wide smile hides lots of teeth — small but sharp.

Work round the outline creating a 'fluffy' effect with petal-like ovals. Circle the eyes with the same pattern as well.

What would you call a monster who ate his mother's sister?

An aunteater!

The fingers are curved with sharp claws, ready to grab!

Fluff isn't a great walker: he's only got one foot. Make the toes comically irregular, with a long big toe and smaller toes to the side.

A few little lumps and bumps on the arms add to the spiky effect.

Knowing eyes and a toothy smirk make it clear that he may be fluffy, but he isn't cuddly.

Minion

Some monsters live in spooky castles, where it is essential that they have at least one creepy servant. That's Minion's job. He's a sort of butler, who is employed by his monster master to bow guests in, though perhaps not out again.

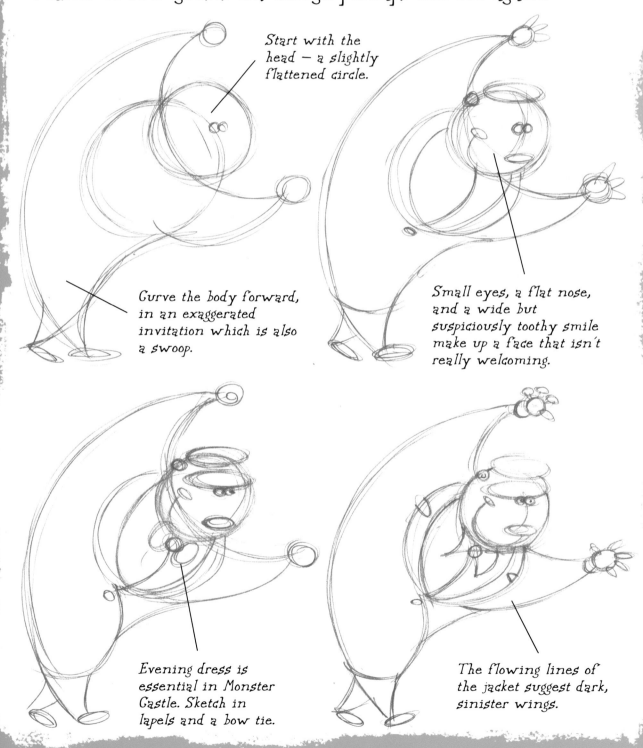

Start with the head — a slightly flattened circle.

Curve the body forward, in an exaggerated invitation which is also a swoop.

Small eyes, a flat nose, and a wide but suspiciously toothy smile make up a face that isn't really welcoming.

Evening dress is essential in Monster Castle. Sketch in lapels and a bow tie.

The flowing lines of the jacket suggest dark, sinister wings.

The single eyebrow forms a curve that bulges out above the lower face.

Continue the body curve down the legs, ending in tiny feet.

Finish drawing the face with a flattened nose, tiny eyes, and a mouth positively frilled with teeth.

Contrast the smooth perfection of Minion's costume with the cragginess of his face.

Did you hear about the vegetarian monster?

He would only eat Swedes. . .and the occasional Norwegian!

There is no need to draw Minion's shadow — his kind don't have them.

Harpy

The Harpy is a monster from ancient Greece who comes to punish wicked behavior. Part woman, part vulture, filthy and smelly, she specializes in snatching sinners' dinners from their tables.

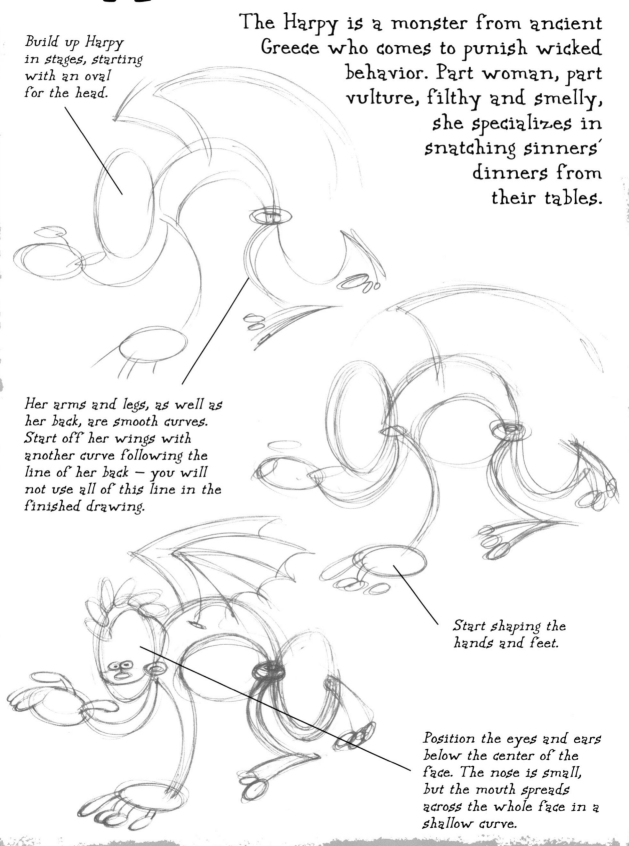

Build up Harpy in stages, starting with an oval for the head.

Her arms and legs, as well as her back, are smooth curves. Start off her wings with another curve following the line of her back — you will not use all of this line in the finished drawing.

Start shaping the hands and feet.

Position the eyes and ears below the center of the face. The nose is small, but the mouth spreads across the whole face in a shallow curve.

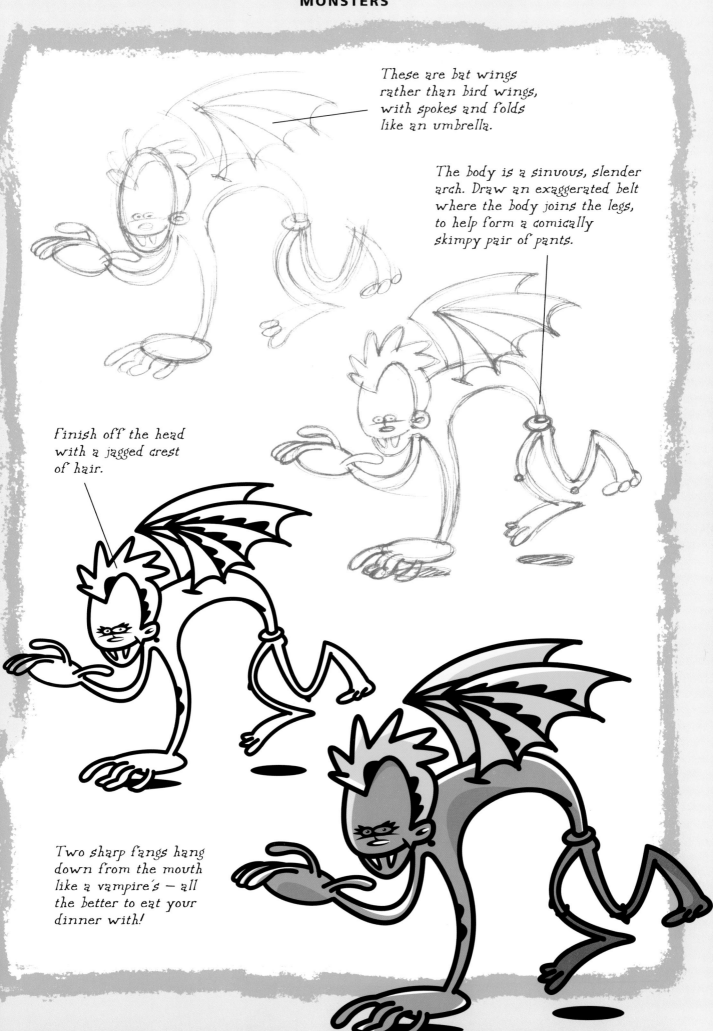

These are bat wings rather than bird wings, with spokes and folds like an umbrella.

The body is a sinuous, slender arch. Draw an exaggerated belt where the body joins the legs, to help form a comically skimpy pair of pants.

Finish off the head with a jagged crest of hair.

Two sharp fangs hang down from the mouth like a vampire's — all the better to eat your dinner with!

G (Sea) Monster

You can make an amusing monster out of any letter of the alphabet: you might find this one in the ocean. In the days when books were written by hand, instead of being printed, some writers used to decorate their capital letters with strange twisted beasts or people. Now it's your turn!

Start with a large capital G — see!

The beast is twisted over, so its head is upside down. You may find it helps to turn your drawing round before filling in the face.

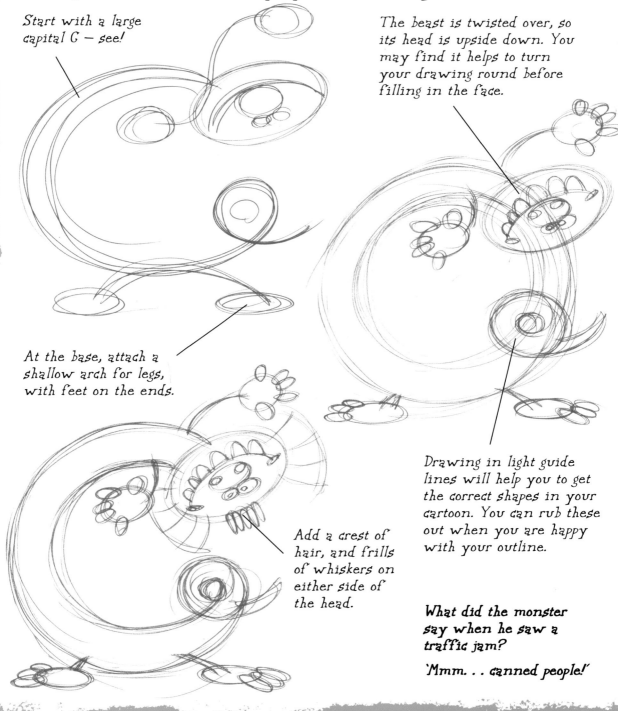

At the base, attach a shallow arch for legs, with feet on the ends.

Add a crest of hair, and frills of whiskers on either side of the head.

Drawing in light guide lines will help you to get the correct shapes in your cartoon. You can rub these out when you are happy with your outline.

What did the monster say when he saw a traffic jam?

'Mmm. . . canned people!'

Keep the arms small, so you don't obscure your 'G' shape.

This is a rather jolly monster. Big eyes and a zany grin give him a happy expression. The hands echo the shape of the head.

The end of the 'G' flows quite naturally into a coiled tail.

When you ink in your outlines, you can add details like whisker spots on his cheeks. A zig-zag pattern down his back and across his forehead add to the overall effect.

When you design an alphabet monster, it's important not to lose the shape of the letter. You can use monsters like this to decorate the words on party invitations and posters.

Godzilla

This giant radioactive dinosaur is a hero of the Japanese film industry. In early films, he is a threat to humankind. In later appearances he is on our side, and saves the human race from a whole host of other monsters.

Godzilla went on a cruise. He went to the restaurant for dinner, and the waiter asked if he would like to see the menu.

'No,' he replied, 'just bring me the passenger list!'

Start with this upturned crescent for the body. Add a big blunt head, marking the position of the eyes.

Draw a second oval overlapping the lower half of the head to help form the mouth.

Draw an arch for legs, and large rounded feet on the ends of them.

Start to form the toes using small oval shapes.

Sketch in a row of scaly plates down the back, and add tiny arms.

Draw in eyes and nostrils, and shape the open mouth with its row of teeth.

Make the hands small and dainty on their tiny arms.

See how the arch you drew for the legs helps you to position them correctly.

Drawing the nostrils like this gives them a raised appearance. Godzilla smells something good!

With those strong legs, feeble hands, and big, broad head, Godzilla is clearly based on the famous Tyrannosaurus.

Golem

A golem is a robot man made out of clay by a sorcerer. He is brought to life by special words written on a paper tucked inside his head. Making pottery is not a skill practiced by many sorcerers, so golems are rarely as good-looking as you or me.

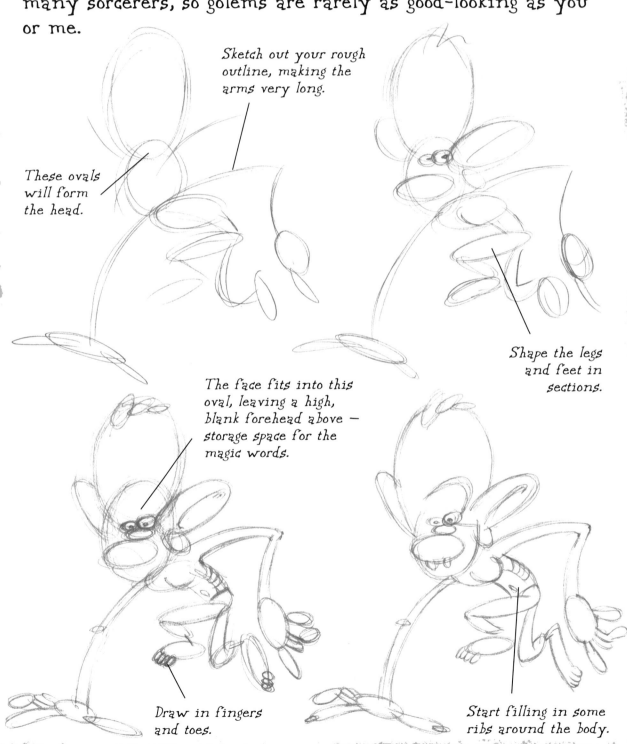

Sketch out your rough outline, making the arms very long.

These ovals will form the head.

Shape the legs and feet in sections.

The face fits into this oval, leaving a high, blank forehead above — storage space for the magic words.

Draw in fingers and toes.

Start filling in some ribs around the body.

A single, large, lopsided eyebrow curves above the eyes.

The fingers are outspread for balance; the thumb juts out backward like a bird's claw.

The golem's other arm is thrown behind him for balance as he prances along.

The ragged pants are for effect, rather than warmth — pottery people don't feel cold!

The golem's feet are big in comparison to his legs — but small compared to his ears!

Flying Saucer

Many people believe that 'Unidentified Flying Objects' seen in the skies are alien spacecraft. They got their nickname of 'flying saucers' in 1947, when an American described them as skipping through the air 'like saucers over water.'

A long flat oval forms the shape of a saucer seen at an oblique angle.

Add a curved line over the top to give the saucer depth. You can see from this shape how some people have managed to fake 'flying saucer' photos using ordinary buttons or lampshades!

Add a smaller oval below, for the base. In movies, this section is often shown opening up to 'beam up' objects from Earth into the craft.

Crown the structure with a domed top, and your spacecraft is almost complete.

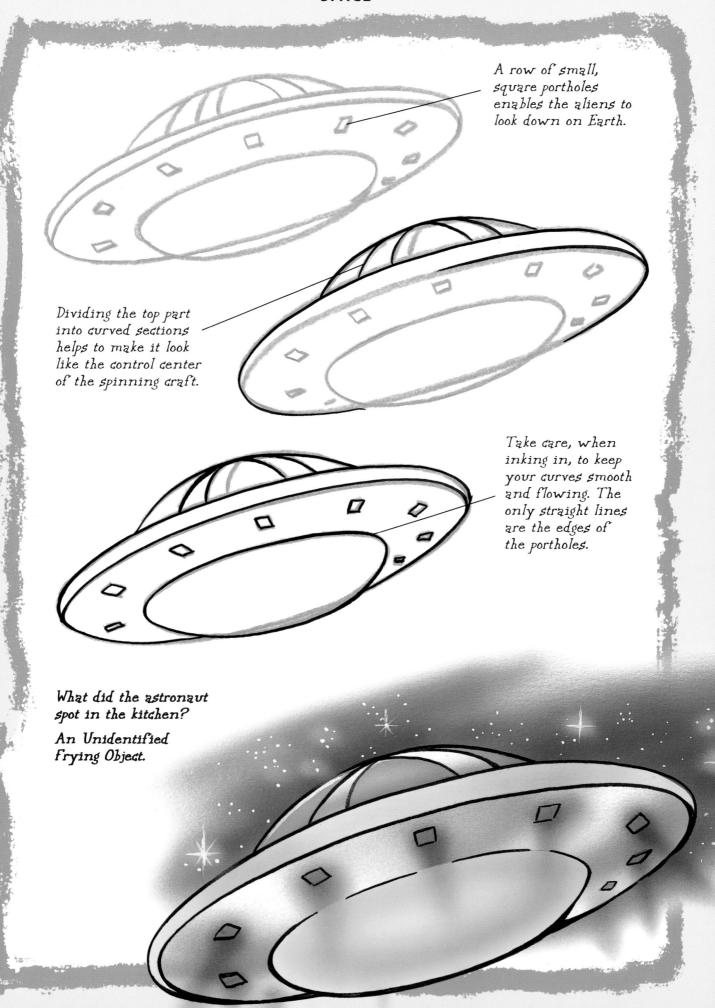

A row of small, square portholes enables the aliens to look down on Earth.

Dividing the top part into curved sections helps to make it look like the control center of the spinning craft.

Take care, when inking in, to keep your curves smooth and flowing. The only straight lines are the edges of the portholes.

What did the astronaut spot in the kitchen?

An Unidentified Frying Object.

Space Shuttle

The Space Shuttle, first launched in 1981, looks a bit like a cross between a jet plane and a rocket. It can make repeated journeys into space and back again — unlike earlier space rockets, that made one trip and then burned up and were destroyed.

Start with this long sausage shape, a bit narrower at this end.

On the side of this shape, add a short, fat wing.

This wing is farther away, so you can't see quite as much of it.

Add the viewing windows of the flight deck — which will double as eyes when you give the Shuttle a face.

Draw the tall tail fin, and a blob at the back for the engines.

In this drawing, the pointed nose cone of the Shuttle is rounded off, to make it look more like a smiling face.

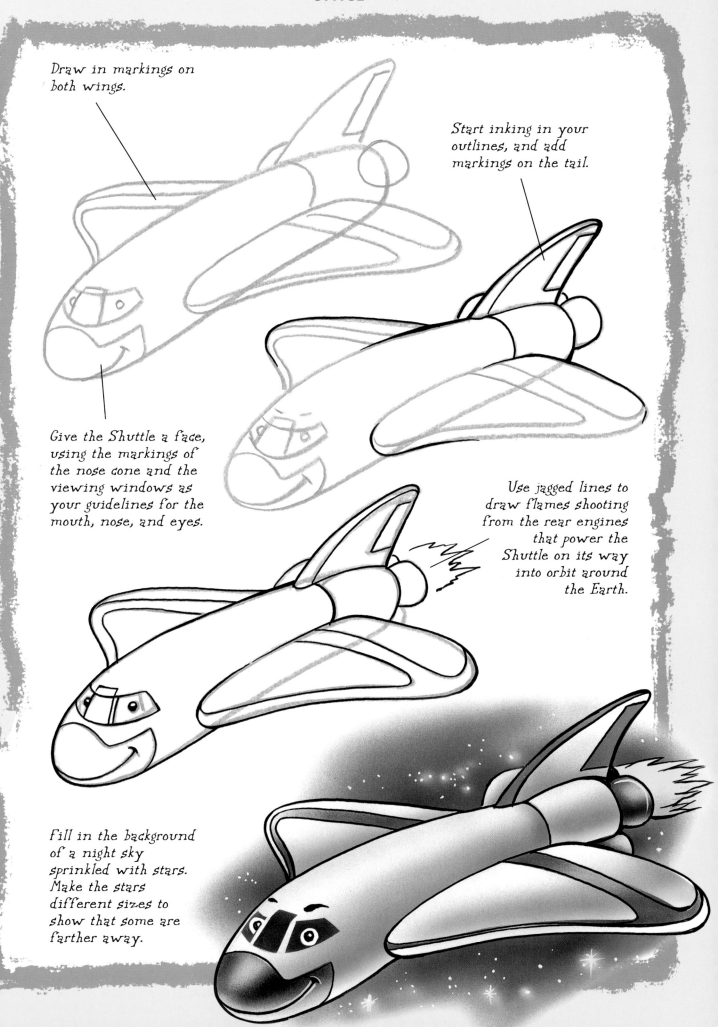

Draw in markings on both wings.

Start inking in your outlines, and add markings on the tail.

Give the Shuttle a face, using the markings of the nose cone and the viewing windows as your guidelines for the mouth, nose, and eyes.

Use jagged lines to draw flames shooting from the rear engines that power the Shuttle on its way into orbit around the Earth.

Fill in the background of a night sky sprinkled with stars. Make the stars different sizes to show that some are farther away.

Exploding Rocket

Space rockets aren't meant to explode. But the fireworks of the same name certainly are. If you put the two ideas together, you can draw a truly spectacular rocket that really does go off with a bang.

Set this rounded shape at the top, so that the two pieces together look like a straight finger with a fingernail at the end.

This long cylindrical shape forms the body of the rocket.

Draw a jagged line about a third of the way down, to mark where the top of the rocket is breaking away from the bottom in the explosion.

In the center, draw a cloud of smoke, with little puffs of smoke to either side. Below this, another jagged line shows where the base of the rocket has broken off.

Add a rounded tail fin on either side of the base.

Add a third tail fin. It looks a different shape because of the angle at which we are looking at it.

Scatter small triangular fragments through the cloud of smoke.

A few small curves within the cloud give it greater depth.

These round shapes form the rocket's engines.

Remember to rub out these guidelines. This part of the rocket has disappeared.

Short, straight 'speed lines' between the shattered rocket and the smoke give the impression of movement.

What do you get if you cross a round black hat with a rocket?

A very fast bowler.

Spacecraft

The age of space exploration has begun — but there are still more spacecraft to be seen in the cinemas than in the skies. This gives you a lot of freedom when it comes to designing your own spacecraft — try this one for a start.

Start with this long oval.

Draw two smaller shapes on either side. These are the boosters, to provide extra power and speed. Be sure to make the one on the left smaller, because it is farther away.

Draw in the viewing window of the flight deck near the front. It is shaped rather like an orange segment. Then add two egg shapes at the back of the craft for the rear engines.

Link up the boosters to the main body of the craft with two broad, wing-like sections. Draw a broad stripe across the back, and start rounding off the curves of the rear engines.

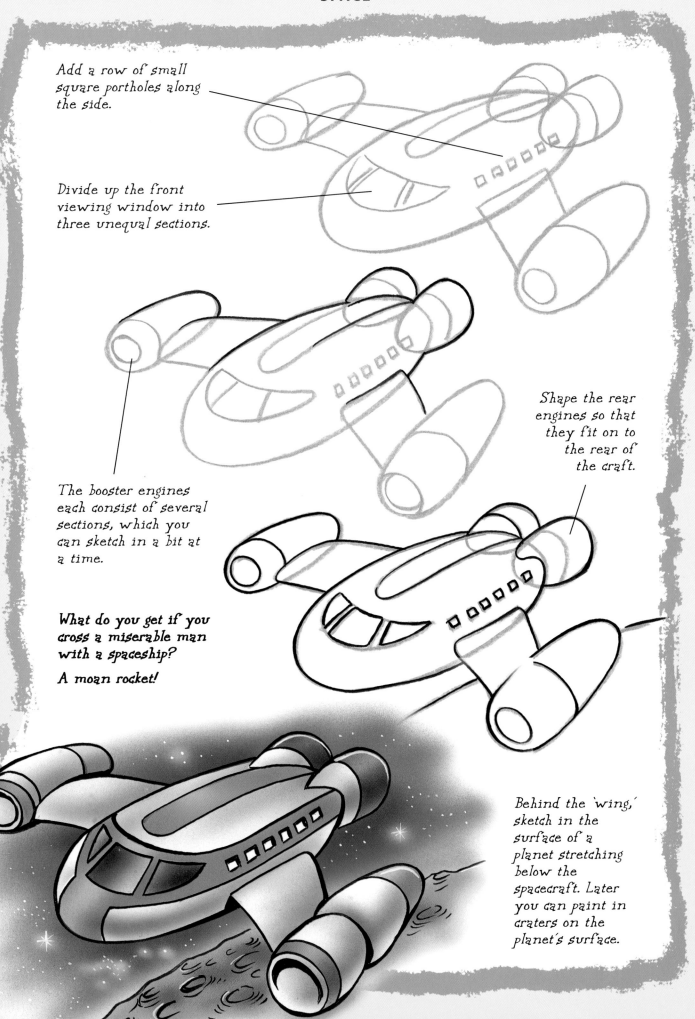

Add a row of small square portholes along the side.

Divide up the front viewing window into three unequal sections.

The booster engines each consist of several sections, which you can sketch in a bit at a time.

What do you get if you cross a miserable man with a spaceship?

A moan rocket!

Shape the rear engines so that they fit on to the rear of the craft.

Behind the 'wing,' sketch in the surface of a planet stretching below the spacecraft. Later you can paint in craters on the planet's surface.

Alien and Spaceman

The contrast between two different figures — here an alien and a spaceman — can be brought out by drawing them in the same pose. Here the two stand facing one another, communicating in sign language — thumbs up!

Five ovals, of varying shapes and sizes, start you off. Be careful to get the proportions right.

Smaller ovals are used to form the man's arms, feet, and oxygen tank, and the alien's feet — all three of them. The alien's neck links up with his head by way of another oval.

Another, interlinked curve shapes the spaceman's arm in its thick, padded sleeve, and a final oval forms his hand.

The alien's skinny, bendy legs and arms match his tube-like neck, and contrast with the bulky limbs of the spaceman in his spacesuit.

Now you can draw in features.
Both figures have similar long
noses and friendly smiles, but
you can have fun making the
eyes very different. The alien's
eyes are placed high and
mounted on stalks

Both characters have simple
hands, and hold their thumbs
up in the same way.

Your curved guidelines help
shape padded sleeves. Use similar
curves to form the legs.

Your alien can be any
color you like — ours is
bright red, but you could
choose green or blue.

**What do you do if you see
a spaceman?**

Park your car in it, man.

Dancing Alien

We usually imagine aliens as being about the same size as us. (It makes it easier to fit actors into alien costumes for movies!) But there's no reason why they should be. This alien could fit into your hand — but he is having much more fun dancing on a spaceman's helmet.

Starting couldn't be easier: just draw two circles, one bigger than the other.

Two more large shapes establish the spaceman's shoulder and arm. Draw another circle for his head within his helmet.

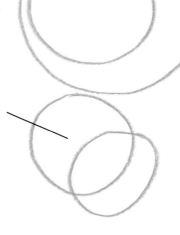

Start drawing the alien, using two small circles. Add a collar and oxygen tube to the spaceman's helmet.

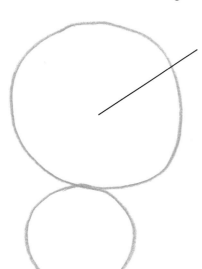

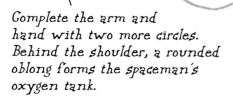

Complete the arm and hand with two more circles. Behind the shoulder, a rounded oblong forms the spaceman's oxygen tank.

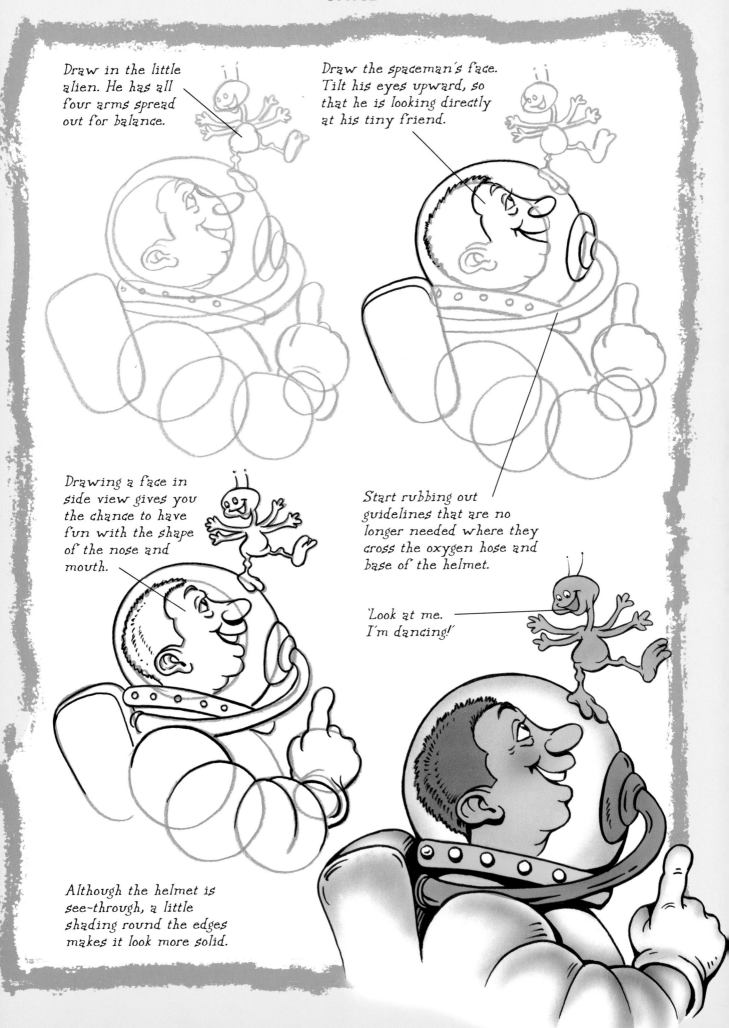

Draw in the little alien. He has all four arms spread out for balance.

Draw the spaceman's face. Tilt his eyes upward, so that he is looking directly at his tiny friend.

Drawing a face in side view gives you the chance to have fun with the shape of the nose and mouth.

Start rubbing out guidelines that are no longer needed where they cross the oxygen hose and base of the helmet.

'Look at me. I'm dancing!'

Although the helmet is see-through, a little shading round the edges makes it look more solid.

Large Robot

If small robots are usually cute or comical (in sci-fi movies at least), big robots are usually more like humans in their shape. In fact, some of them look quite like walking suits of armor. They may be friendly or sinister, depending on your taste. This one looks harmless!

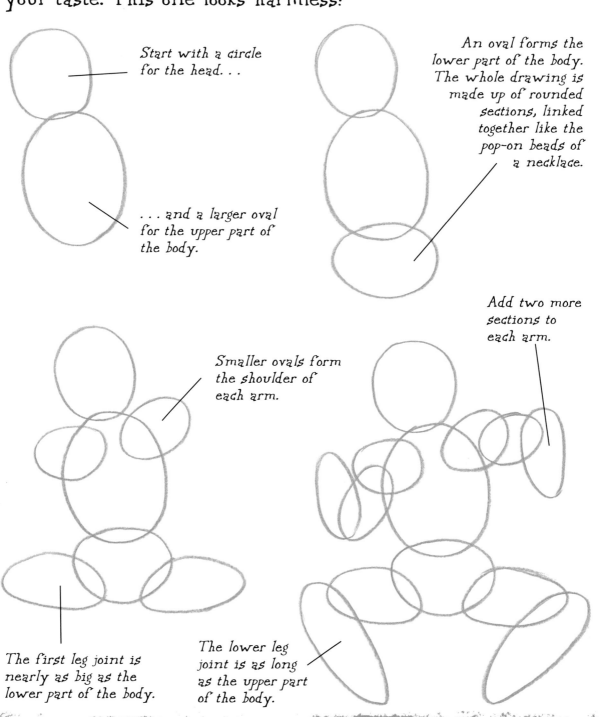

Start with a circle for the head...

... and a larger oval for the upper part of the body.

An oval forms the lower part of the body. The whole drawing is made up of rounded sections, linked together like the pop-on beads of a necklace.

Smaller ovals form the shoulder of each arm.

Add two more sections to each arm.

The first leg joint is nearly as big as the lower part of the body.

The lower leg joint is as long as the upper part of the body.

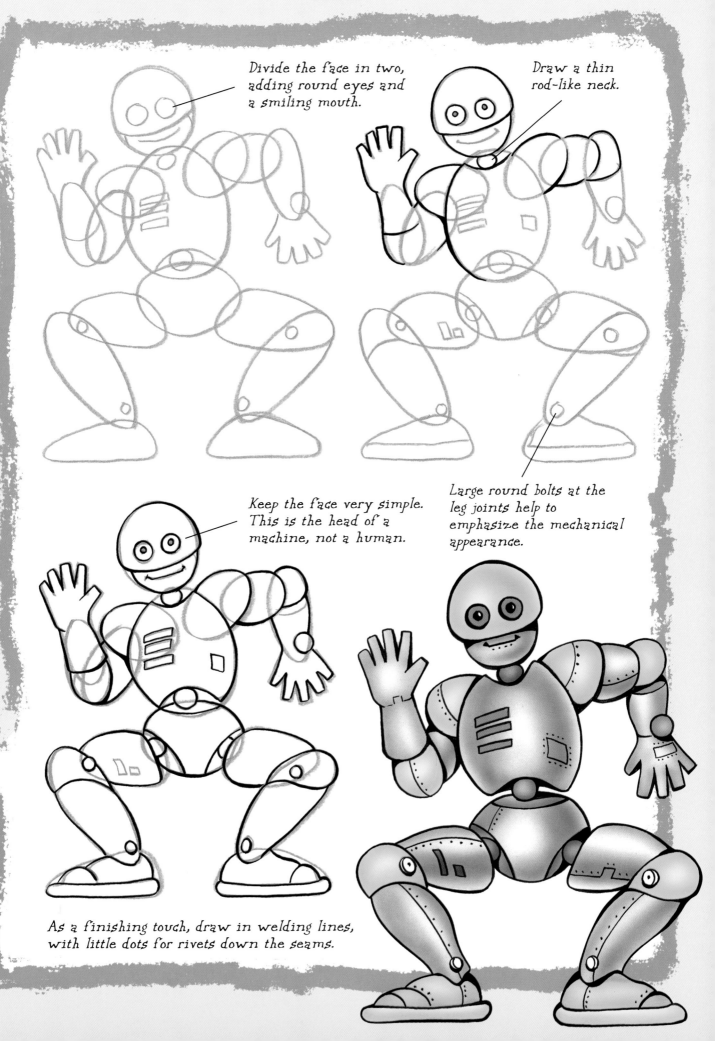

Divide the face in two, adding round eyes and a smiling mouth.

Draw a thin rod-like neck.

Keep the face very simple. This is the head of a machine, not a human.

Large round bolts at the leg joints help to emphasize the mechanical appearance.

As a finishing touch, draw in welding lines, with little dots for rivets down the seams.

Two-headed Alien

There's no reason why an alien should have the same number of heads as humans. Two heads are supposed to be better than one! That may be true when the two heads manage to agree, but this guy seems to be having problems!

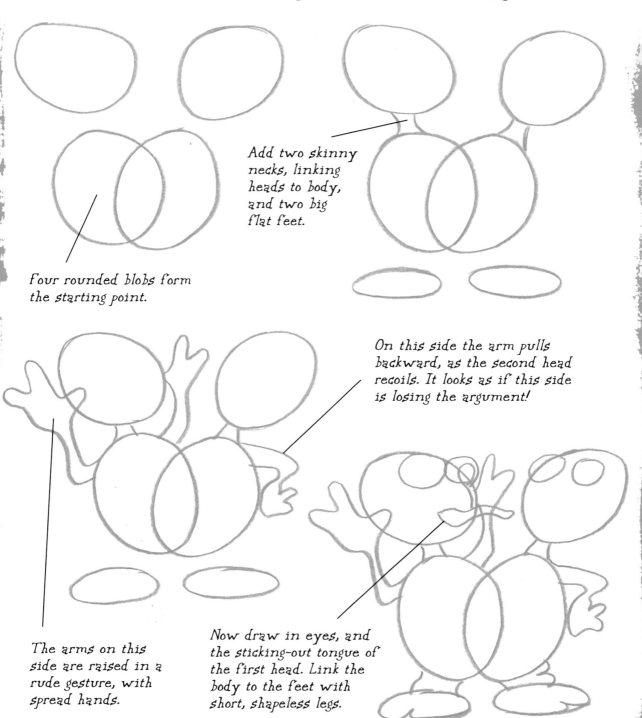

Four rounded blobs form the starting point.

Add two skinny necks, linking heads to body, and two big flat feet.

On this side the arm pulls backward, as the second head recoils. It looks as if this side is losing the argument!

The arms on this side are raised in a rude gesture, with spread hands.

Now draw in eyes, and the sticking-out tongue of the first head. Link the body to the feet with short, shapeless legs.

Finish drawing the faces. Small changes to the original guidelines for the heads will enable you to bulge out cheeks and narrow chins, making the heads more expressive.

The expression in the eyes tells the story.

The guidelines where the two original body shapes overlap are no longer needed. Let the two bodies merge into one lumpy form.

The shape of the hands is less important than the gestures they are making. The hands themselves can be quite roughly drawn.

Why does an alien always buy clothes at a ridiculous price?

Because he has to buy them for an absurd figure.

What did the alien say to the librarian?

Take me to your reader!

Teacher

One way of getting across a sense of character is to concentrate on the head. Making it much bigger than the body emphasizes the expression, as in the case of this stern teacher.

This drawing is made up of strict, straight lines. Start with these two boxes.

More straight lines build up the body and legs and mark out the blackboard. Start shaping the head by cutting off the corners.

Two curving lines across the face establish the site of eyebrows and mustache. Take care with these, for they form the basis of the expression.

Shape the trousers, and add tiny feet. Use short lines to pinch in the body at the waist

Draw the small arms and hands, and start adding detail to the jacket. Use the curve of the mustache to help shape the large nose.

Sketch in the eyeglasses and the rest of the face. The eyes peer over the top of the eyeglasses to give the class that piercing look we all know so well.

Drawing the body leaning toward the blackboard makes a more interesting picture than if the body were standing stiffly upright.

Ink in the eyebrows, lowered over the eyes in a frown, and the stern mustache. Frown lines beside the mouth add to the expression.

One foot is seen sideways on, but the other is turned toward the viewer, and therefore looks shorter.

Did you hear about the cross-eyed teacher?

He couldn't control his pupils!

Girl Scout Leader

Another way to caricature people is to draw them ridiculously short and squat. This is a good way to draw bossy people who always tell you what to do — like teachers or scout leaders. It takes away their authority.

Take care with the angles of this shape.

Add two little stick arms.

Two slanting lines mark off her baggy shorts. A short slanting line at the top will form the top of her beret.

Add hands, giving this one a long pointing finger.

Draw in the head, and run a line down the center of the body.

Sketch a comic face, and give her a clipboard to hold.

Draw block-like shapes for the feet.

Make the hair wild and straggly — this woman doesn't worry about her coiffure!

Now draw in her uniform, adding details like breast pockets and badges.

In cartoons, figures of authority always peer over the top of their eyeglasses. The prim little mouth and upturned piggy nose make an entertaining contrast.

Our Girl Scout Leader certainly watches her weight. She has it out in front of her, where she can see it!

Emphasis is laid on the square face and the uniform of huge, baggy shorts and bulging blouse. But the arms, pointing instructions, and solid, sensible legs also work to comic effect.

Chef

An expert at work is impressive — except when he's in a cartoon, when something always seems to go wrong. Cooking a chicken is easy for a chef; but suppose he had to catch the chicken first? 'Stop that bird!'

Seven short lines give you the basis of head, hat, and body. Cartoon chefs always wear the tall white hat that is the mark of their trade.

Three more short straight lines form arms outstretched to grab the bird.

Running legs are easily sketched in with this zig-zag line.

Add detail to the arms and legs. Now you can sketch in the chef's face, using his hat as a guideline to position the nose and ear.

In front of the arms, draw this egg shape for the chicken's body.

Working outward from the egg-shaped body, draw in the chicken. A round eye, looking backward at its pursuer, and wide-open beak give it a comic look of alarm.

Make sure the chef's hands are lined up with the fleeing bird.

Give the chicken a comb and wattles, feathers on tail and wings — and a trail of feathers behind!

The chef's fingers are spread wide to catch the elusive bird.

His white jacket needs very little extra detail — just add a row of buttons.

'Spin lines' in front of the chef's foot, and long, bold speed lines behind both figures increase the sense of movement.

What do you call someone who's eaten one of the chef's specialties?

An ambulance!

Tourist

Everybody finds the stupid tourist a comic figure. Tourists wear loud shirts they would never wear at home, and usually have cameras glued to their faces. Of course, that's not true when we go on holiday — we are tasteful tourists!

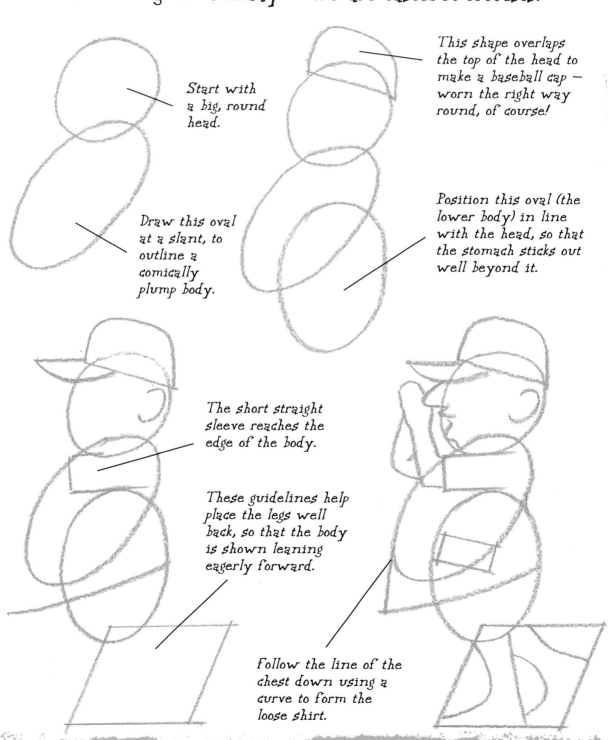

Start with a big, round head.

This shape overlaps the top of the head to make a baseball cap — worn the right way round, of course!

Draw this oval at a slant, to outline a comically plump body.

Position this oval (the lower body) in line with the head, so that the stomach sticks out well beyond it.

The short straight sleeve reaches the edge of the body.

These guidelines help place the legs well back, so that the body is shown leaning eagerly forward.

Follow the line of the chest down using a curve to form the loose shirt.

Fill in the face with chubby cheeks, smile, and sunglasses — and don't forget the video camera!

Use the back of the slanted oval to establish the line that the strap of his camera still follows over his shoulder.

A few simple lines create the sandals.

Smooth out the outlines as you ink them in, so that shoulders and back form chubby curves.

Brightly patterned shirts like this are the uniform of the tourist in cartoons — and often in real life!

Mister Angry

If the next-door neighbor shouts at you for breaking a window, his anger isn't funny. But if he stamps his foot and screams in a temper tantrum, it is. When grown-ups behave like children, it's a cartoonist's dream!

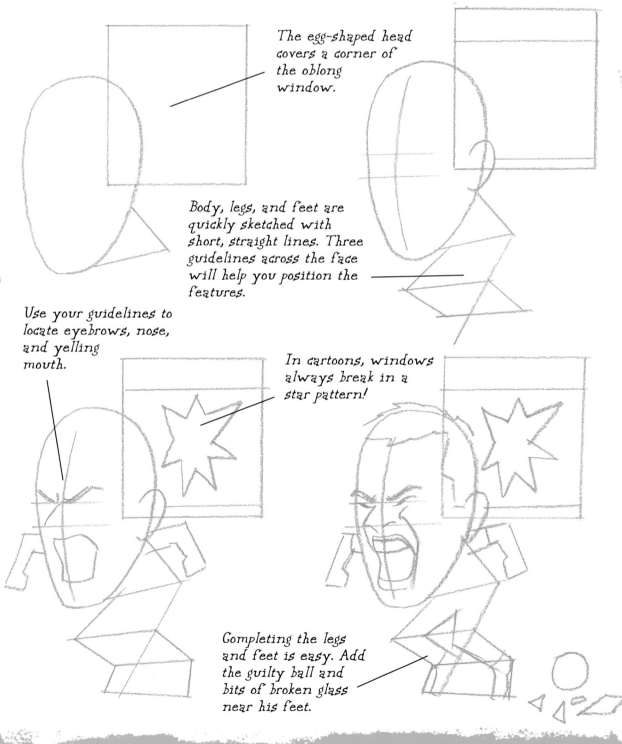

The egg-shaped head covers a corner of the oblong window.

Body, legs, and feet are quickly sketched with short, straight lines. Three guidelines across the face will help you position the features.

Use your guidelines to locate eyebrows, nose, and yelling mouth.

In cartoons, windows always break in a star pattern!

Completing the legs and feet is easy. Add the guilty ball and bits of broken glass near his feet.

The eyes are slanting slits. Grease lines beside them show that they are screwed up in rage.

A striped shutter at the top, and a sill at the base, make it clear that this is a window. It's all done with a few straight lines!

Draw in the upper teeth — the lower set need only be suggested.

Uneven jagged lines make a more convincing hairline than straight ones.

Short curved 'spin' lines below fists and feet help to give life to the picture.

First man: Why are you so angry?

Second man: Oh, it's all the rage these days.

Rugby Player

Cartoons characters are simplified. They usually have either brawn or brains — not both. Rugby players need muscles, so cartoon versions are always big and thick — in both senses! Lack of brains is suggested by a low forehead and heavy, ape-like jaw.

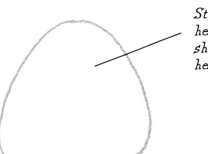

Start with this heavy, domed shape for the head.

These two ovals form the body, tipped forward because he is running, and the all-important rugby ball.

Attach this leg section to the back of the body. An oval for the other leg is placed a little distance from the body.

Complete the legs and feet. The legs are stretched further apart than we could manage in real life, to show that the player is running flat out.

This arm and hand clutch the ball tightly to hold it in a firm grip.

The other arm is stretched out in front of him, adding to the impression of the speed of this human battering ram.

Draw in the facial features, curving the lower lip outward to emphasize the jutting, determined chin.

Rugby shirt and shorts are easily sketched in, following the lines of the body.

Be generous with your speed lines.

Exaggerate the size of the shirt collar for comic effect.

Color in his kit with your favorite team strip — and look out anyone who is in the way!

Policeman

Uniforms help to identify your characters. Cartoon policemen nearly always wear flat hats — because these are recognizable as police uniform in many different countries around the world.

Start with the oval head, and draw a dividing line down the center. Add two horizontal guidelines.

This even-sided diamond will contain the arms and body.

Use your central line to position the nose and a large, sweeping mustache. Add a pair of big ears and add detail to the hat.

Arms and legs are easily drawn following your guidelines.

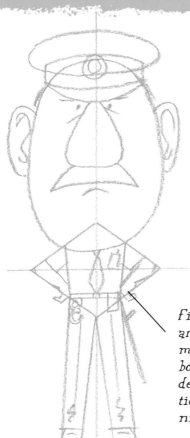

A disapproving expression is created with small eyes and mouth, both dwarfed by the huge nose and mustache.

Finish drawing the arms and hands, and make the legs end in boots. Add other details like the tie, radio, and nightstick.

Another important detail that helps to identify the policeman are the handcuffs hanging at his belt.

Keeping the face simple allows us to concentrate on the 'What's going on here?' glare. In contrast, the small, neat body in its uniform is drawn in more detail.

Policeman: 'I'm going to have to lock you up for the night.'

Suspect: 'What's the charge?'

Policeman: 'There's no charge, sir. It's all part of the service!'

Jumping Jill

Although actions like jumping feel jerky and sudden, they can be drawn with smooth, flowing curves. This drawing is based on a simple scaffolding of three bold curves. Shapes like head and feet are built up on these lines.

Two ovals form the head and hair.

Start with this framework of flowing lines.

This large foot points downward as she springs up on her toes.

Sketch in the T-shirt as a rough bell shape. Use small ovals to mark out the loose hem, neckline, and armholes.

You don't need to worry about drawing arms and legs with realistic joints. Draw them thin and bendy, like pipecleaners, to suggest freedom of movement.

A curved line across the face helps you to place the eyes.

Keep the face simple with a button nose and smiling mouth. Add a ponytail flowing out behind.

Large hands look less fussy than small fiddly ones.

Rub out the guidelines as you draw in the T-shirt and leggings.

Cartoon characters always have big feet — easier to draw as well as more comical than small ones.

When you have finished erasing your guidelines, most of the original 'scaffolding' lines are hidden. They have done their job in forming a smooth, flowing shape.

Keep clothes simple, so they do not distract attention from the movement. The bold shading produces a lively visual effect.

Snowballing

Clothes are important in cartoons as well as actions. People playing in the snow need to dress up warmly. The bulky clothing sets your scene just as much as the snowball itself.

Warm winter boots make for great big feet. A second oval alongside the foot marks out the top of the boot.

Draw in the wide smile, even though most of it will be hidden by the coat collar.

The body is fat and rounded in its thick jacket.

Build up your cartoon using ovals and curved lines to suggest movement.

With one leg high in the air, the body leans backward, putting all its power into throwing the snowball.

Drawing both legs as a single curved line looks odd at this stage. But this is only a guideline to help you eventually to draw the legs at the right angle.

The lower part of this circle becomes a hand, with fingers curved around the snowball.

Only part of the face appears between hat and jacket collar.

Add detail to the jacket and sleeves with a series of ovals to create the padding.

The zigzag line of the jacket zip follows the curves of the jacket. Don't forget the zip tag!

Use bright colors for your snowballer's winter clothes.

There's no business like snow business!

Time for Tennis

Tennis is a game that many players take very seriously. Try to draw the effort that goes into following the ball, and the player's total concentration on the action. It's supposed to be fun, but here it looks more like hard work!

Use smooth, flowing curves to suggest movement. Roughly position ovals for the head, hands, feet, and racket.

Nearly all the lines lean the same way, as the player strains to one side to try to hit the ball. His free hand curves the other way to help keep his balance.

This small circle will form the tennis ball.

Strong curves — semi-circles, in fact — shape the bent legs. All the weight of the leaning body is balanced on one foot, while the other swings upward.

The face turns toward the ball, so its features are not central but shifted to one side.

Clean up your guidelines and start to smooth out your outlines.

Suggest the racket strings with a few criss-cross lines.

The ball is coming just over his head, toward the racket.

Hands can be very expressive. Here the fingers and thumb are flung out widely as the player strains toward the ball.

Board Rider

This skateboarder is confident that he has mastered all the tricks of his sport. He's leaning with the board on a radical ride, grinning happily. Drawing the board at an angle with flattened wheels gives the impression of speed.

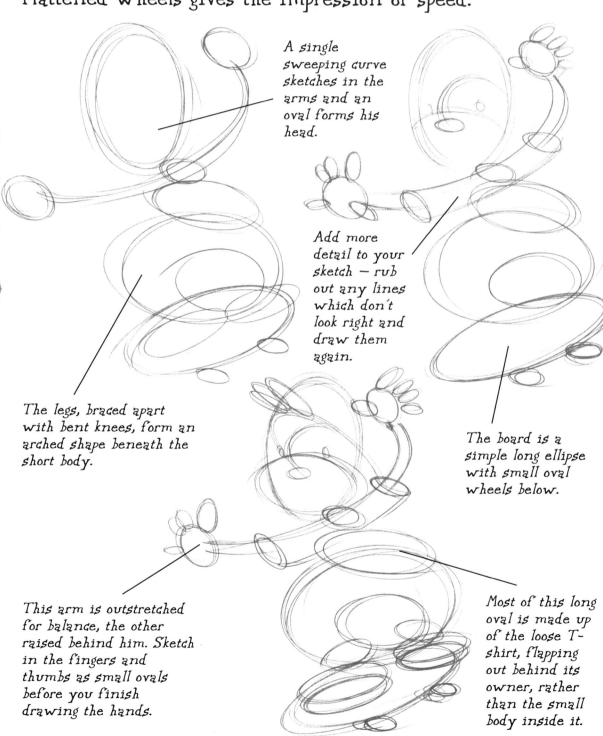

A single sweeping curve sketches in the arms and an oval forms his head.

Add more detail to your sketch — rub out any lines which don't look right and draw them again.

The legs, braced apart with bent knees, form an arched shape beneath the short body.

The board is a simple long ellipse with small oval wheels below.

This arm is outstretched for balance, the other raised behind him. Sketch in the fingers and thumbs as small ovals before you finish drawing the hands.

Most of this long oval is made up of the loose T-shirt, flapping out behind its owner, rather than the small body inside it.

Start drawing in the face in more detail.

Add a wide grin. This is cool!

Draw in the big boots, heels together.

Fill in the body, and the flare of the T-shirt behind.

Clumps of hair fly out through the front of the reversed baseball cap.

Ink in the outline — add solid shadows to give your cartoon more definition.

Draw the skateboard wheels at an angle to show speed.

Most of the guidelines remain as final lines in this drawing — not too much rubbing out! Now you can add bright colors.

Handstand Harry

It's no good drawing someone standing upright, then turning the paper upside down! You need to convey the effort that goes into the exercise. Most people, when doing a handstand, bend their bodies and legs — especially if they're not expert gymnasts.

Draw the feet pointing in different directions.

The body leans over to one side. Draw it loosely using flowing lines.

A shallow oval at the base of the head will help you to form the chin.

Use your curving guidelines to draw in the bent legs.

The egg-shaped head doesn't quite reach the floor — leave room for hair hanging down. Sketch in the curve of the smiling mouth.

Now add the hair, hanging toward the ground and almost filling the space between the arms.

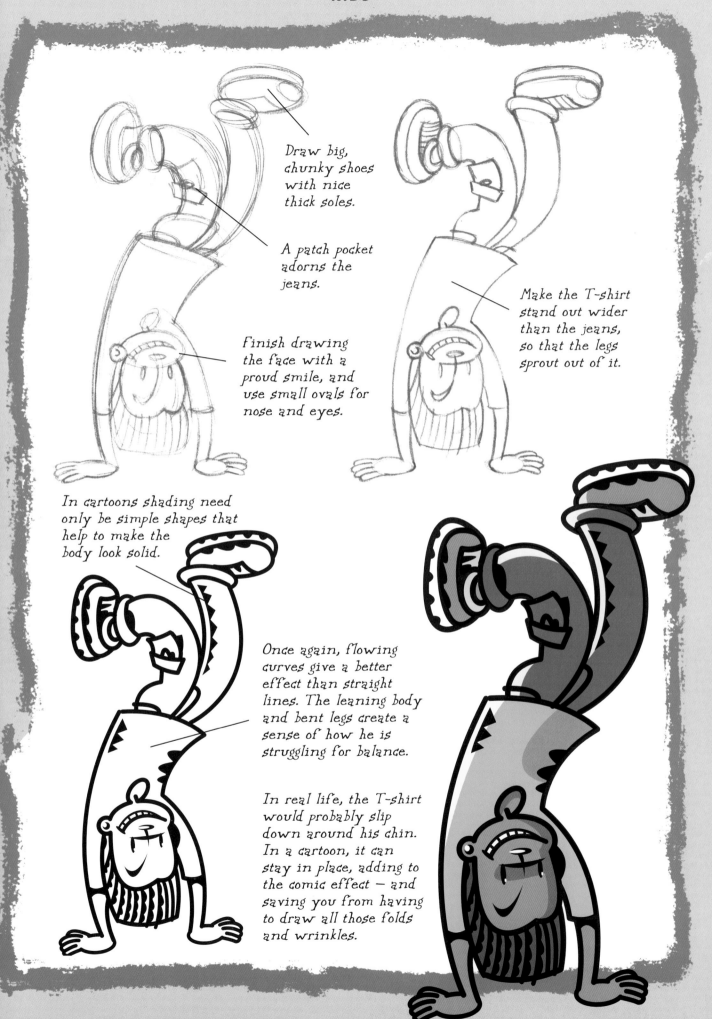

Draw big, chunky shoes with nice thick soles.

A patch pocket adorns the jeans.

Finish drawing the face with a proud smile, and use small ovals for nose and eyes.

Make the T-shirt stand out wider than the jeans, so that the legs sprout out of it.

In cartoons shading need only be simple shapes that help to make the body look solid.

Once again, flowing curves give a better effect than straight lines. The leaning body and bent legs create a sense of how he is struggling for balance.

In real life, the T-shirt would probably slip down around his chin. In a cartoon, it can stay in place, adding to the comic effect — and saving you from having to draw all those folds and wrinkles.

Scooter Sue

Scooters aren't the fastest thing on two wheels. But this rider obviously thinks she's racing along. You can create the impression of speed by making the rider lean back, with her hair streaming behind.

Set the circle for the body just behind the head and legs.

The scooter is easily sketched — base, wheels, and handlebars. Place two big feet firmly on the base.

Sketch in a simple, smiling face.

Link the body circle to the legs with a couple of small ovals, to create a rounded, curved shape.

Sketch in the short, sturdy legs, bent backward to maintain balance. The effect is that the body is being dragged along by the speeding scooter.

Now you can start to draw the face and flyaway hair.

Add detail to the hair — spikey at the front, and streaming out smoothly behind. Don't forget, you can rub out guidelines as your cartoon takes shape.

Use your guidelines to draw in the small wheels. You don't need to attach the front wheel to the scooter — just curve a wheel arch above it.

Make the T-shirt extra wide, so that it streams out behind too.

Now you can ink in your outlines using smooth curving lines. Simple black shapes will create shadows and creases.

Pop, can I have an encyclopedia?

Certainly not, you can walk to school like all the other kids!

Unicycle

Riding a unicycle takes a lot of skill, and a good sense of balance. But it's more fun to draw someone whose sense of balance is a little wobbly! It probably isn't a good idea to lean quite this far backward in the saddle!

Set the head well over to the side away from the wheel. Use curved lines and oval shapes to plan your drawing.

Draw in the center of the wheel so that the pedal will fit under the foot.

Sketch in ovals for the feet at the top and side of the wheel.

Check the position of the legs. They start safely enough directly above the wheel, then curve boldly back toward the tilting saddle.

The hair forms a circle, following the curve of the outflung arm and interlocking with the oval of the face.

Making the face broader below the eyes gives a cheeky, monkey-like expression.

Hands can be drawn using simple shapes.

Follow your rough guidelines to draw in the rider's clothes.

Start to form smooth outlines as your cartoon develops.

Draw the back of the saddle peeping out behind the rider.

Add highlights to the eyes, and spiky eyelashes.

Break up the smooth fall of the hair with a few floppy locks.

Clean lines and black shading will bring your cartoon to life.

Riding a unicycle is wheely difficult!

Juggling Jack

Juggling is easiest when you use a set of similar objects. To make it more interesting, this juggler is managing to spin a hoop on his leg at the same time as keeping all the balls in the air.

This circle forms a guideline for the two legs. You can rub out the lower half of the circle later, when you no longer need it.

A shallow oval across the lower part of the head helps you to shape the mouth and jaw.

Draw in big round hands, and an oval to mark out the path of the flying balls.

Draw in six balls, using your oval to help you plot their path up and down.

The body (drawn the same size as the head) slants toward the busy hands and the cascade of balls.

A curve around the eyes marks out the position of the eyebrow.

Draw the arms rather long, because they are reaching out to catch the balls.

Use small ovals to sketch in the legs of the shorts, and the tops of the socks.

Position the hoop whirling around the leg. You could add 'spin' marks to show that it is moving.

The hands are slightly curved, with outstretched fingers, to catch and throw over and over again.

Why shouldn't you take a vampire to the circus?

Because he always goes straight for the juggler's vein!

Big, boat-shaped shoes give the juggler a firm base to stand on.

Gone Fishing

Hunting and fishing were the caveman's version of going shopping. Of course, it was a bit more dangerous. This cartoon takes a humorous look at one of the risks a prehistoric fisherman might face . . .

Two small interlocking circles start off the figure of the fisherman.

Sketch in the monster's gaping jaws. Add a little oval between the jaws for the small fish, and a blob on the water for the fishing float.

This big sweeping curve forms the monster fish's head.

Thick, bent legs set well apart start turning your two circles into a man.

Finish shaping the man, with his arms stretched forward to hold his rod. A line beneath the figure gives him the shore to stand on.

Give the little fish a tail, and the big fish lips and eyes. In real life, most fish have round eyes, but in cartoons it's more fun to draw a glaring human-shaped eye.

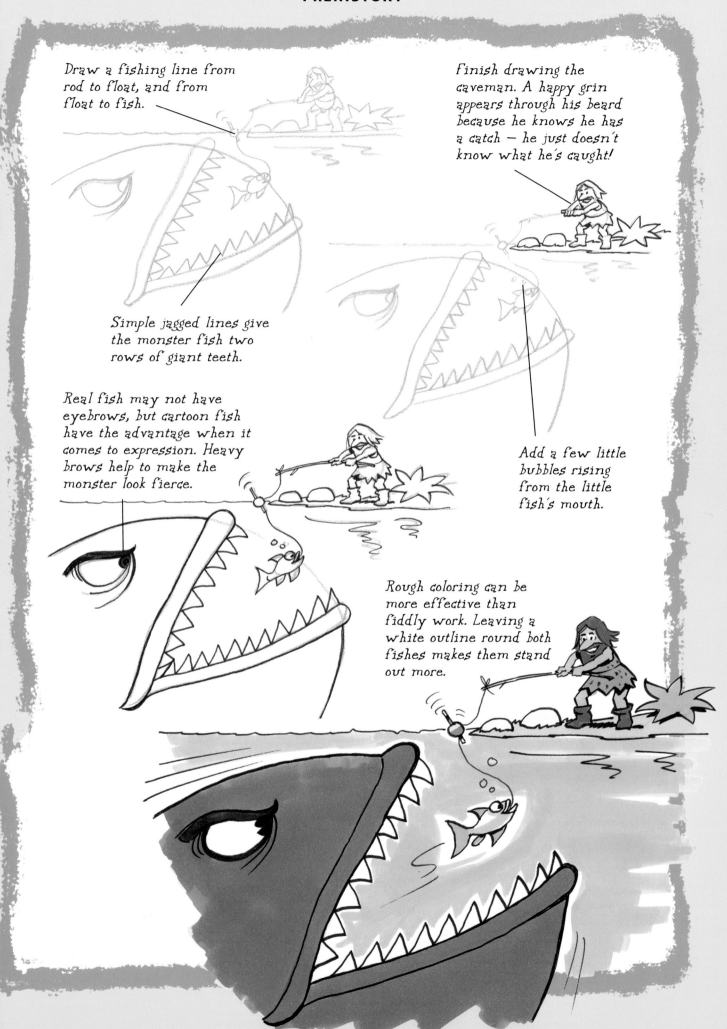

Draw a fishing line from rod to float, and from float to fish.

Finish drawing the caveman. A happy grin appears through his beard because he knows he has a catch — he just doesn't know what he's caught!

Simple jagged lines give the monster fish two rows of giant teeth.

Real fish may not have eyebrows, but cartoon fish have the advantage when it comes to expression. Heavy brows help to make the monster look fierce.

Add a few little bubbles rising from the little fish's mouth.

Rough coloring can be more effective than fiddly work. Leaving a white outline round both fishes makes them stand out more.

Prehistoric Mailman

It's a favorite joke among cartoonists to imagine the Stone Age as being just like ours, but with everything made out of stone. Of course, there would be problems. Imagine having to deliver letters carved on slabs of stone!

This big slab covers most of the mailman's body.

Build up the cart with back, wheel, and a slanted shape for the stack of rocks — I mean letters.

Draw the side of the cart first, on a slight slant. Make sure you set it far enough away from the mailman to leave room for the cart's handle.

Fill in the shape of the mailman clasping his heavy load. His hands are spread out, clutching the stone slab. Add three simple curves on top of his head to form his peaked cap.

Finish drawing the rest of the cart and the stack of stone slabs. Add a small wheel at the front of the cart, and a wooden handle so the mailman can haul it along.

Draw in the wooden framework of the cart.

Screwed-up eyes, puffed-out cheeks, and pursed mouth show the huge effort involved in carrying rocks. Increase this impression with 'spin' marks to show how the postman is wobbling under his load, and sweat drops flying from his face.

Details show how the cart is made, with stone hub caps on the wheels, and criss-cross ties at the wooden joints.

A few rows of short straight lines represent Stone Age handwriting.

Mailman: 'I've had to walk three miles to deliver this letter to your farm.'

Farmer: 'You should have mailed it instead!'

Courting Couple

The cartoon world has its own rules, whereby certain characters always behave in the same way. In this world, dogs always chase cats, fat people are always funny — and cavemen always woo their women with a club, and drag them home by the hair.

The man's head and body are the same size, the body slightly slanted.

Add arms the same length as the body. Sketch in the legs, making them very short and set close to the ground.

Draw his woman's head a little distance away.

Sketch in lines for her legs and upturned feet.

Link her head to his hand with this tapering shape for her hair.

Now you can complete her outline, making her slimmer and lighter than her mate . . .

. . . and finish drawing him. Sketch in his long hair, beard, and mustache.

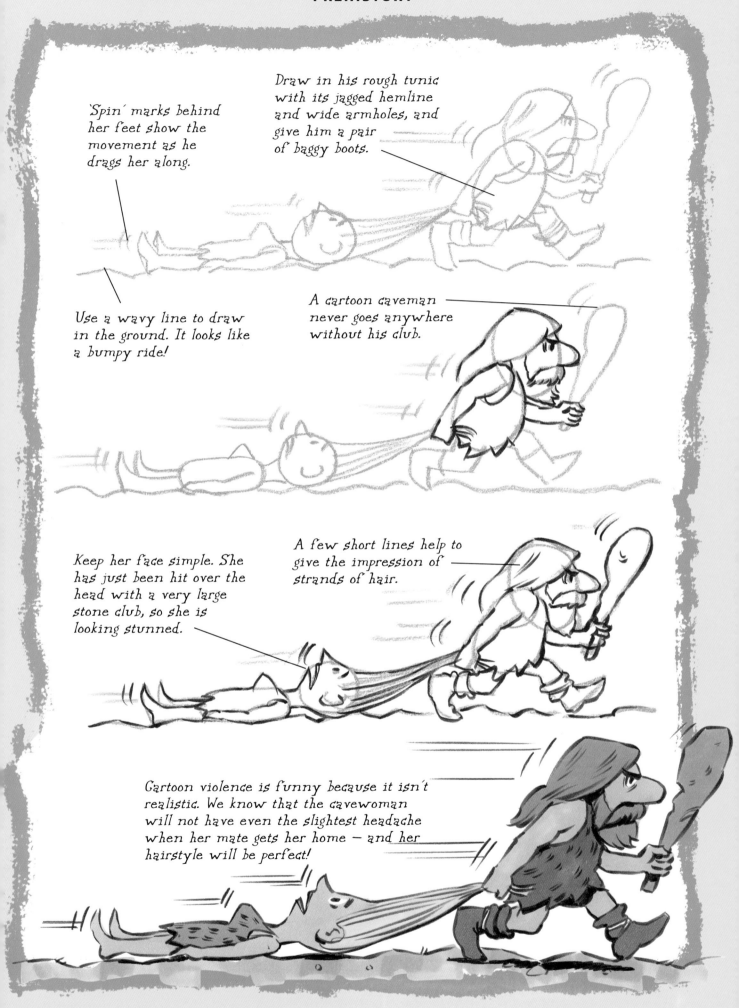

Pushing the Baby

Simple everyday objects seem comic in the cartoon Stone Age. A baby carriage with massive stone wheels and a leaf canopy is instantly amusing. Silly details, like the baby's toy dinosaur and his mother's handbag, add to the fun.

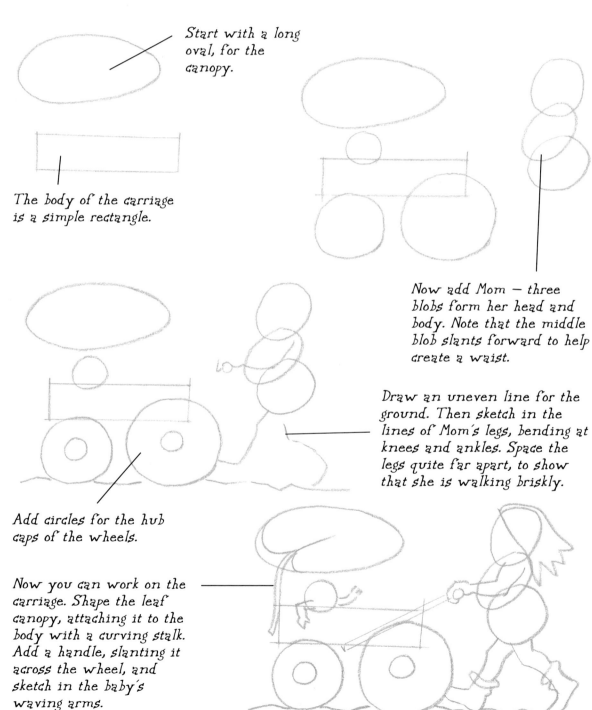

Start with a long oval, for the canopy.

The body of the carriage is a simple rectangle.

Now add Mom — three blobs form her head and body. Note that the middle blob slants forward to help create a waist.

Draw an uneven line for the ground. Then sketch in the lines of Mom's legs, bending at knees and ankles. Space the legs quite far apart, to show that she is walking briskly.

Add circles for the hub caps of the wheels.

Now you can work on the carriage. Shape the leaf canopy, attaching it to the body with a curving stalk. Add a handle, slanting it across the wheel, and sketch in the baby's waving arms.

Stone Age Mom wears a simple short dress with jagged hem, lumpy boots, and a shaggy hairdo. She is not so very different from a real-life modern mother — as her handbag reminds us.

The baby looks directly at us, beaming and waving his toy dinosaur.

Curve her fingers around the handlebar.

Curved 'spin' marks near the wheels show that the carriage is rolling along.

Cartoon babies have an instantly recognizable 'uniform,' consisting of a big head, a tuft of hair on top, and a single tooth. They are always either crying, with huge open mouths, or smiling widely. This mother is lucky!

Don't forget to show how the primitive baby carriage is held together. Criss-cross lines show where the pieces of wood, and the leaf canopy, are tied in place.

Earthmover

We all know that humans and dinosaurs were not around at the same time. But in the cartoon world, they were! This allows cartoonists to find some unusual uses for dinosaurs.

Two circles form the head and body of the rider (or driver, if you prefer!)

Start with a big square for the dinosaur's head, and an egg-shaped body a little way away.

Use short, straight strokes to sketch in the big jointed legs.

Within your guidelines, create a slanting forehead and massive open jaws.

The tail is as thick as the neck but longer, tapering toward the end.

The driver's face consists mainly of nose and beard.

Give the dinosaur an eye and zig-zag teeth. Then draw in the earth which this living earthmover is shoveling up.

Finish off the feet with rounded toenails, and add little creases at the leg joints.

The driver's seat is a simple structure made of pieces of wood tied together. Use a ruler to mark out its straight lines.

You can see here two different ways that guidelines work. The oval sketched for the dinosaur's body is still recognizable. But the head square is only a frame for the head and jaws, and it will be rubbed out.

Make sure the neck curves smoothly to the shoulders.

In the absence of control buttons, this driver has to work his 'machine' with hand commands.

The driver wears standard caveman 'uniform' of animal-skin tunic and boots.

Nobody knows what color dinosaurs were, so you can choose any color you fancy. You can even copy the colors that your local construction firm uses for its earth-moving machinery if you like!

Doomed Dinosaurs!

Another approach to cartoons is to look at the facts about a subject in a new way. Everyone knows that dinosaurs died out. But let's imagine one of the dinosaurs knew what was going to happen. Would the others have believed him?

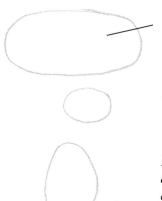

This oval forms the dinosaur's placard. Carefully spaced beneath it, draw smaller ovals for head and body.

Big, fat legs bulge out on either side of the dinosaur's body. Add the stick supporting his placard.

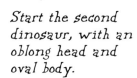

Start the second dinosaur, with an oblong head and oval body.

Continue work on the first dinosaur. Complete his body with a narrow chest, and sketch in wide blocks for his feet. Add a plump, tapering tail.

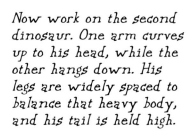

Now work on the second dinosaur. One arm curves up to his head, while the other hangs down. His legs are widely spaced to balance that heavy body, and his tail is held high.

The dinosaurs' expressions are important. The placard holder looks understandably worried, with downcurved eyebrows and mouth.
But the other's brows and mouth slant upward — he's laughing his head off.

But this dinosaur is up on his toes in a bouncy position — he's not worried. He taps his own forehead as if to say, 'You're nuts!'

The first dinosaur's claws curve round his placard stick, clutching it tightly to himself. His whole demeanor looks miserable.

'Spin' marks draw attention to the movement of his hand.

THE END OF THE WORLD IS NIGH!

Late for Work

Things that happen every day in real life make great cartoons when drawn in a different setting. You've seen people hurrying to work in the rush hour. How would a caveman cope with this? He wouldn't have a fast car!

Two rounded shapes form the rider's head and body. Make his body slant slightly, so that he is leaning back in the saddle.

The dinosaur's head and body are long ovals, spaced well apart to allow for the neck.

Turn your two ovals into a man by adding arms and legs. One arm swings forward to hold the reins, while the other swings back to drive his mount on. Below his foot, draw an oval for the top of the dinosaur's leg.

The long, tapering tail curves slightly upward toward the end.

Link the head and body with a long neck, growing wider toward the chest.

The slim legs are at full stretch. Notice how the back foot curves upward as it swings up from the ground.

Give the dinosaur a face, and mark out the noseband of the simple bridle.

Draw in the rider's face.

A whirlwind of speed marks shows that the dinosaur is in top gear. A few puffs of dust behind him add to this impression.

The tiny front legs are tucked up out of the way

Most of his face is hidden by a beard, so the grim expression is created by wide eyes under heavy brows, and a downward droop to the mustache.

Add detail to the rider's clothing — a fur tunic with jagged edge, and big boots.

Don't forget to add more speed marks behind the rider.

The dinosaur's toes aren't drawn in detail — so they look blurred with speed.

Public Transport

If one man can ride a smallish dinosaur, you can easily get four on a big one. It's simple enough to turn a giant dinosaur into a bus. But perhaps it isn't quite so easy for the Stone Age bus driver to get his vehicle to move!

A big oval forms the huge body. Position the small head some way away and a bit lower down.

A row of four blobs along the dinosaur's back will become its passengers.

Draw a small 'snowman' for the bus driver's head and body, just in front of the dinosaur. Set it a little higher, to leave room for legs.

Four more blobs build up the passengers into 'snowman' shapes. Give the dinosaur four thick, short legs.

Join head and body with a long, tapering neck.

Now give the driver arms and legs. His left arm is bent close to his face.

Sketch in the passengers' arms and legs. Beneath their feet, a long line establishes the framework of their seats.

Start drawing in details of the driver. Lowered eyebrows help make him look annoyed. 'Spin' marks round his pointing hand help show his impatience.

Draw in the framework of the bus seats, with the driver's empty seat at the front.

The dinosaur's jaws close round a mouthful of grass. Lowering his eyelid across his eye helps to make him look comfortable, settling in for a good meal.

Make the passengers look really fed up. They've paid for their seats, and now the bus won't move! The front passenger is shouting something down to the driver.

The fact that the driver is looking at his watch, worrying about the bus timetable, adds to the humor.

Most of your original guidelines are no longer needed. Rub out the sections of the first oval here.

I waited ages for a number 22 bus. But it never came.

What did you do?

Well, eventually two number 11s came. So I got on them instead.